D1565035

The Incredible Secret Money Machine

by
DON LANCASTER

Howard W. Sams & Co., Inc.
4300 WEST 62ND ST. INDIANAPOLIS, INDIANA 46268 USA

Contents

this book is dedicated to the quest for the perfect tinaja

All opinions expressed are solely those of the author.

Find Out How I Make Money - Send Five Dollars And Ninety Five Cents to...

If this was one of those get-rich-quick books, we would probably start out by telling you how many zillions of dollars I am making and how I need a wheelbarrow to haul it daily to the nearest bank.

Well, I don't use a wheelbarrow. The rattrap carrier on my five-speed bicycle works just about as good, and there's no point in going to the bank every day, particularly since it is closed on weekends. And, no way am I into zillions of dollars. Just into the fractional megabucks, nothing more. At least just yet. But it's something I can live with for the time being.

All of this good stuff is done with my incredible secret money machine. *Your* incredible secret money machine is your own small computer, craft, or technical business. Done within the guidelines of this book, your incredible secret money machine can make you filthy rich beyond your wildest dreams.

We are going to look at lots of the nuts-and-bolts details of getting your money machine off the ground and flying right side up. That's what this book is all about. But, before we even start, there's a few entrance requirements we have to agree on. Here are the basic beliefs you must have to build your money machine on:

first, you have to be heavily into a technical or craft trip on a total lifestyle basis.

The absolute single most important thing in your life has to be doing something technical or artistic in a better and a different way than anyone else. You can decide what the trip is—it can be action-in-motion photography, low-cost hobby computer hardware, improving weaving looms, doing quality printing and presswork, developing sanely priced small business computer software, building furniture, developing alternate energy systems, sailing, ceramics, robotics, underground housing, portraiture, blacksmithing, community access communications, or just about anything else that is both highly personal and creative.

Your own trip has to be the absolute center of everything you do, everything you work with, and everything you believe in. Doing it has to be much more important to you than making money, more important than worrying about what people think, and more important than behaving, competing, or complying the way that others think you should.

second, you must want to stay in control.

You have to feel that everything in your money machine reflects you and that purposely keeping the scale of your money machine small is the only way to keep in control. This means you won't want to spend much of your time hassling others, reporting to others, or competing with others in any way, shape, or form. For your money machine to work, you have to want to spend much of your time, energy, and effort improving both yourself and the general goodness of the technical or craft trip you are into.

third, your income goals should be just enough to keep going

Getting filthy rich should be nowhere in your plans. So long as you can continue doing what you like in the direction you want to go, that's all that should matter. The great irony of your incredible secret money machine is that the *less* you strive for income, the *more* of it will come your way, and, more importantly, the *more* you will be able to do with what you already have.

Any time or effort spent directly toward making money is time not available for your main trip. This is wasted time and energy that eventually hurts you rather than helps.

fourth, you have to be gentle.

Your incredible secret money machine has to be gentle on yourself, gentle on people, and gentle on the environment. Your money machine should be forever small and decentralized. It should never compete head-on with others. It should complement and advance what others are doing. Your money machine's products should genuinely help people at a fair or more-than-fair price, never being a ripoff either to suppliers or to customers. If your particular money machine is into high technology, make sure it is *appropriate* technology used only when it clearly and genuinely is the best approach to what you are doing.

and so . . .

Unless you are willing to let these four beliefs be the foundation of everything you do with your money machine, very little of this book will work for you.

Let's see if you can't second guess some of what we're going to show you about your money machine by taking a simple quiz.

If your money machine is to be based on our four guidelines, which of the following do you think are important?

	Essential	Not Important	Avoid at All Costs
Adequate advance financing	☐	☐	☐
Aggressive marketing	☐	☐	☐
Creative management	☐	☐	☐
Solid patent protection	☐	☐	☐
Tight employee security	☐	☐	☐
Practicing the business of business	☐	☐	☐
Good high traffic location	☐	☐	☐
Strong legal and financial advice	☐	☐	☐
Heavy use of other people's money	☐	☐	☐
Total new product secrecy	☐	☐	☐

Now—and I hope you are ready for this—score yourself one point for each "avoid at all costs" box, and zero for everything else. A passing score is +10.

Surprised? That's why the whole incredible secret money machine idea works. We'll see why everything on this list is very bad for your money machine, as is much more of traditional business advice. Since our four basic guidelines are vastly different from the "do unto others before they do unto you" philosophy common to much of the business world, it's no wonder that we need a different set of rules. As we'll see in the next chapter, having enough advance financing is the absolute single **worst** thing your money machine can have.

Let's go on and take a much closer look at your incredible secret money machine. We'll first check into the key strategy and tactics secrets, followed by ways to get started and to keep informed. From there, we'll go on to communications, both words and pictures. I am personally very heavy on communications, since that is the key to my own money machine. After that, we look into some unmatters, tax dodges, and a final look at "investments," whatever they are.

As we go on, you'll find that this is a book of contrary opinion whose main point is that doing the exact opposite of traditional beliefs and advice usually lets you end up far ahead. Everything here either works or seems to work for me. I believe and follow pretty much everything we're about to look at.

Now, admittedly, it may be that my own money machine works *in spite* of some of this rather than because of it, but I'm not about to change things to find out.

Many of the ideas we'll be looking at are not mine, but are borrowed from people I believe in. For instance, you'll find lots of the small-is-beautiful of Schaumacher and Callenbach, and much more of the appropriate technology of Brand and Baer. Conviviality belongs to Illich, while the intelligent ignorance concepts are from Kettering. Anything far off belongs to the Batwing Hamburger Snatcher. Do-more-with-less, of course, is pure Fuller. And granfalloons are a Vonnegutism.

By the way, nothing is made up. All examples and ideas are based on real people running or getting run over by their own real money machines.

So . . . . Onward and upward.

Or, far off.

Or whatever.

Your incredible secret money machine only will work if . . .

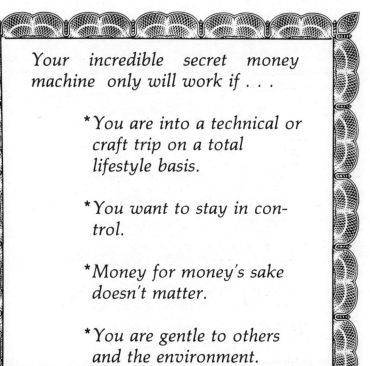

      You are into a technical or craft trip on a total lifestyle basis.

      You want to stay in control.

      Money for money's sake doesn't matter.

      You are gentle to others and the environment.

"Sit anywhere. We're equal opportunity employers."

ONE

Secrets I – Strategy

You can call any larger, long-term detail of getting your money machine in gear a *strategy*, while an everyday fine point is a *tactic*. In chess, checkmating the king is the ultimate strategy, while concentrating your power toward the center is an intermediate strategic goal. A move of "pawn takes queen, check" might be a good tactic or might not, depending on the skill of your opponent.

Your money machine is driven by a combination of the strategy and tactics of this and the next chapter. Not every principle will apply to every money machine. The incredible secret money machine belonging to a free lance science author is obviously going to differ from that of a stained glass artisan, and both of these will differ from the machines belonging to a computer art freak or a graphics designer.

But, as you look around yourself at the incredible secret money machines of others, you'll find that the better running machines use as many of these secrets as possible. So, let's turn to some strategy first:

strategy secret—have as many different sources of income as possible.

You can call them customers, clients, users, patrons, or anything you like, but any money machine will need a continuous source of nickels to keep running. At the beginning, you have a choice of having one humongous source of nickels, several smaller sources, or bunches and bunches of very small sources that add together to handle the care and feeding of both you and your machine.

Having only one source of income is so incredibly stupid that we won't even talk about it here. Whatever that single source is, it will

11

certainly be using you to its own profit, having you do what it wants rather than what you want yourself and your money machine doing. It may even insist on such dumb things as your being at a certain place at a certain time, wearing specified costumes, or paying tribute to others in its hierarchy. It may even think it is giving you security or that it owns you in some way.

Several different sources of income are much better. It's usually easier to find ten places to scrape up a thousand dollars a year than one that can get you ten.

But, your money machine will work best of all if it has hundreds or, better yet, thousands of tiny sources of income. There are several good reasons for this.

No customer will think he owns you if he is one among unwashed thousands. Customer expectations will also usually be lower since they are probably dealing in a smaller way with you. Your customers will only come to you when they genuinely think they need you, rather than figuring out things for you to do to keep you busy all the time.

Better yet, if you can get enough small customers, they will start to obey the statistical laws of large numbers. This means you will be able to predict future sales and cash flow with good accuracy. And, should you lose a customer or two, it's not too bad if there's lots of others left over. Those same laws of big numbers will warn you when you are about to lose bunches of customers—and maybe even suggest what you are doing wrong as well.

Eventually, several of the smaller customers will become bigger ones that take up more and more of your money machine's product. This is fine when it happens, but it is not something you want to aggressively go after when you are starting out. The important, even crucial, point is to never let any one customer dominate your money machine to a point where he is in control.

Should you ever end up with one very large customer and many small ones, arrange your money machine and your whole lifestyle to live within the nickels generated by all the smaller sources combined. Force yourself to be *independent* of the income generated by the biggie. Funnel this extra single-source income into improving your money machine, into the "investments" of the final chapter, or into having fun—but always keep this extra income separate from your bread-and-butter smaller income sources.

Sometimes, working through a few major customers can't be helped. This is obviously the case with a book, unless you self-publish. When this happens, make sure your major customers in turn base *their* sales or their customers on many small sources. Having many clients or customers yourself is best, but having them "once removed" is still a workable route.

strategy secret—have complementary sources of income

You can call this the "if the right one don't get you the left one will" approach. Arrange your money machine to give you at least two products or services that behave differently with regard to the effort you put in and the nickels you get back. Here's some real-world examples:

* combine a print shop with a specialty direct-mail bookstore
* merge a paperback book exchange with a copy service
* write user-oriented textbooks and design electronic kits
* silk screen funky T-shirts, signs, and electronic PC boards as well as being the only local litho service
* provide custom millwork along with authentic replication of 17th century furniture
* be both the best sign painter and the best auctioneer in town
* offer wilderness guide service along with trail map sales and free-lance wildlife photography
* run a photo studio in combination with a beginner's photography school and by-the-hour darkroom rentals

and, no way could I make this one up . . .

* combine a transcendental meditation temple with a firewood hauling service

Each of your complementary activities should cover the weak spots of the other. One may be low profit or low volume but steady and sure. Another may be very rewarding and pay very well, but take extensive time or effort. Or be seasonal or high risk.

This complementary idea is nothing new. A car dealer may offer new cars, used cars, car repairs, a body shop, financing, and fleet leasing services. Each reacts to economic conditions in a different way. Title companies and realtors always seem to be next door to each other, as do insurance outfits and savings-and-loan institutions. In all these cases, all bets are hedged with complementary sources of income.

Eventually, one of your complementary money machine parts may take over and dominate the rest. This is fine and almost unavoidable, so long as it happens well *after* your money machine is started and running well enough that a hedge is no longer needed. Most often, the part of your machine that takes off will surprise you. It rarely will be the exact direction you started out in. This points out another reason for the complementary sources—to expose yourself to as many possible directions for your money machine. Once you are inside your own money machine, reality will assume a new perspective and change rapidly, so you'll want to expose yourself to as many options as you can.

Your complementary income sources can be just about anything. Often, the further out they are, the better they will be for you. But, there is one super-important limitation to what you pick for your complementary sources. Remember that the first and most important goal of your money machine is to be into some technical or craft trip on a total lifestyle basis. Everything you do should aim directly at this goal. Ideally, all your complementary sources should do this for you.

At the very least, any and all nickel sources should be consistent with your beliefs, goals, and lifestyle. Under *no* circumstances should you ever be into anything just for the money.

strategy secret—*always work toward deferred income*

What you do for your money machine should generate nickels both today and tomorrow. You should work toward automatically guaranteeing yourself a long string of future nickels that needs little or no more attention from you.

This is admittedly very tricky to do, but if you can pull this off, your money machine will fly by itself, freeing you in the future to do bigger and better things.

Book royalties are a good example. Once you've written the book, it can generate income for years on end, without much further attention on your own. Manufacturing royalties for electronic kits are another route to future nickels, but this tends to be riskier, much shorter, and has a far lower return. Software tapes for retail computer store distribution are a new and largely unexplored way to bring future nickels to your doorstep.

There's more subtle but equally important ways to do the same thing for just about any money machine. Simply arrange things so your customers or clients will want to return for more. This is an obvious route toward some future income.

Working out an art technique and perfecting it so that future products will be simpler and easier to do is another example. For instance, if you are into computer art, getting your software up and running, finding a plotter, and getting decent first-time results will take lots of time and effort. But, once your "front end" effort is complete, generating new artwork and copies in the future is a matter of loading the right random numbers, or even letting the poor computer draw everything it knows and then picking only the good ones.

Drafting a set of underground housing plans, how-to details on a solar cooker, or alternate energy system research may also take a lot of front end time and effort. But once this effort is done, there are long-term plan sales, stories and articles, kits, assembled units, teaching opportunities, products that expand on what you have already done, and even T-shirts and posters.

It's always a good idea to hedge your bets by having your present effort work toward *several* future income goals. A hobby computer product development can be several magazine articles, a technical paper, a design contest entry, a book chapter, a kit design for a manufacturer, a thesis or project for a school course, and a way of training yourself for more and better things. Besides all this, it should also be a challenge and a lot of fun.

Always look for at least a "two tone" approach to the time and energy you put into your money machine. Do things that pay you reasonably well now, but that also have the long-term potential to generate nickels on their own without much further help.

strategy secret—have as much personal value added as you can

Your personal value added is the extra effort, energy, and time you put into your money machine that makes the difference between what goes in the hopper at the top and what comes out the bottom. For your money machine to work, your personal value added has to be far and away the single most important part of your final product.

As a ferinstance, let's talk about an ordinary piece of typing paper.

If you are running an office supply store, you can make a penny on this piece of paper. That penny reflects the difference between the wholesale price and your selling price. Your personal value added here consists of what you put into making your store attractive and in how you relate to your customers.

If, instead, you are running a typing service, you can now buy the paper for a penny and sell it for fifty cents or more. Now, you have over fifty times the return since your personal value added consists of putting information on paper just the way the customer wants you to.

Things get much better if you make up the words yourself instead of using those somebody else already wants. A medium length story in a larger magazine should pay you several hundred dollars for a dozen or so sheets of paper. This will average out about ten dollars per page, another 20:1 improvement.

Put the paper into a book manuscript, and the sheet can be worth several hundred dollars to more than a thousand dollars per page, providing it's a run-away best seller like this one.*

And, if you are into consulting, critiquing, or ad copy, your words can be worth as much as $25 to $50 *each*. Let's see, at 225 words per page and 500 pages per ream and $50 per word, that's . . . you figure it out.

In each example the sheet of paper is the same. The only difference is the personal value you have added to make up the difference between the bare paper input and the out-the-door nickel-fetching result.

Maximizing your personal value added protects you in many ways. If what you are offering is basically a part of you, no way can any large corporation compete successfully against you. For that matter, it should be hard for *anyone* to go one-on-one against you, for everyone has his own way of doing things and his own way of looking at products.

Should inflation change the cost of your materials and supplies, this will only have a negligible effect on your selling price if the bulk of your added value is your own doing. You'll never be forced to "cut costs" by going to inferior materials and supplies if your total costs are a very small part of the value of what you are providing.

Computer software, particularly for the hobbyist market, is another example of a product that is almost pure personal value added. So is auctioneering. So are most forms of teaching and instruction. So is just about anything artistic where the final selling price very much exceeds the basic materials cost.

Note particularly that your personal value added must be *directly* a part of what goes out the door. Hassling or "managing" people in no way provides any added value. Nor does time spent in "marketing," whatever that is.

strategy secret—get in control of information flow

Raw information is the highest energy stuff there is. It's also the easiest thing to add lots of personal value to. You should aim at being your customer's cheapest, best, and most useful information source.

---

*There is no point in writing a book if it's not a run-away best seller.

This is easy to do if you are on any electronics trip. Many manufacturers have traditionally avoided putting any useful information out for students, hobbyist, and other small scale users, except on a ripoff basis. Most often, they bury anything useful in trade journals, data sheets, ap-notes and technical papers that the average student never heard of and has no easy access to. The little he can get his hands on is often shallow, out of date, confusing, and misses the mainstream. It can be dull and lack vibes to boot.

Herein lies a gold mine. If you first find and then gather the really useful and current information from these obscure sources and then put it into a lucid and clear form your customers want and can understand, you're almost certain to have a successful money machine. You'll be providing a tremendous service and generating lots of nickels as well.

Offering a course, running a school, or simply teaching others one-on-one are other very good ways to get in control of information flow. The measure of how well you do this is how well your students feel you are giving them useful information in the most interesting way at the best possible price to them.

Your own control of information can make you a better craftsperson, offering more value added in your products, even if you aren't directly selling information to your customers. Even gathering the information sources of others and putting them in one place can be very effective. If you have available all the ceramics books there are or stock all the alternate energy books, you're well on your way to control of the information flow process. When stocking the work of others, completeness and the right overall vibes are keys to your customers seeking you out for specific help.

In any case, always find ways to gather information from obscure or diffuse sources, concentrate it somehow, and then put it into a lucid and clear form that you or your customers can use. Always make the cost of a customer getting information from you far lower and far more pleasant than his using any other source.

strategy secret—put nothing between you and your customers

When you sell a product from your money machine, it should go *directly* to the customer. There should be nothing messing up or otherwise coloring the sales channel, particularly another person or a specific location.

Free lance authors meet this secret the easiest. They write their story anywhere and anytime they like and then mail it to a magazine or book publisher they think wants it. If they called their shots right, a check comes back, or maybe even bunches of monthly checks. The only thing the publisher goes on is your product itself. No way is where the product originated or how it was pushed on them by someone else an influence in the process. Five years and fifty thousand dollars worth of material later, the author may or may not drop in on the publisher who may or may not buy him a Big Mac with cheese. The author's needs are directly met on his own terms with an absolute minimum of outside influences.

Crafts people will have a little harder time meeting this goal of a clear channel between supplier and user. One very good approach to selling pottery, weaving, glass art, paintings, and so on is to find a very high energy and very occasional channel that will strongly attract customers. Arts and crafts fairs, street booths, exhibits, conferences, and shows are obvious routes. The high energy channel will pull in both direct sales and all-important contacts for future sales and exhibitions. The combined presence of other exhibitors will attract far more people than you could by yourself. Similar possibilities include co-ops, guilds, and artisan lofts.

An approach that works very well for hobby computer hardware is direct mail. This is an obvious route to any sale of a hardware or information product. Direct mail is very good for things like kits, where the final user will have extra added value of his own to put in the finished product.

With direct mail, you make your product known as best you can through a limited and very specific amount of advertising. You combine this with as much "free" advertising you can snarf in the form of product releases, technical articles, papers, word of mouth, club presentations, and so on. You then handle the products on an order-and-ship basis.

There are lots of advantages to direct mail. The lack of a retail mark-up lets your products sell at much lower costs. Buy decisions are self-generated and highly motivated. Rarely will the customer think he was "sold" anything, especially if your advertising is honest, your delivery immediate, and your prices reasonable. In fact, immediate delivery of an electronic or hobby computer product will so completely blow your customer's mind that he won't believe it.

Any retail store location with its expensive fixtures, finance charges, fixed overhead costs, and hired help, simply isn't needed. Nor is the whole image trip that goes with it. Always avoid your own retail location and any type of "sales" or "agent" or "marketing" associates of your own. In cases where you have to go a retail route, carefully pick the stores of others on a direct or consignment basis, and always do it on your own terms. Try to work with other money machines where you can. Always be in tune to whether the *final* purchaser or user receives fair value for the products generated by your money machine.

strategy secret—have 0.834 employees

Employees are a hassle, a waste of time and money and a psychic energy sink. You should avoid them at all costs.

Your incredible secret money machine should have 0.834 employees—that is 83.4 percent of you, nothing more, no less. The remaining 16.6 percent of you should go for fun and rewind time. Spend much less time on your money machine and the job will never get done. Much more and you'll be grinding yourself down.

The instant you add an employee, you add an incredibly inefficient and noisy mind-to-mind communications channel that dramatically lowers the efficiency and potential of your money machine. On top of this is the hassle of paperwork, tax and other regulations, and scheduling so your employee is busy just enough of the time to be worthwhile.

So, if you have no employees, how do you get the things done that you don't have time for, don't want to do, or "know" that others can handle better? As much as possible, you should handle these things by buying or trading specific services from other money machines, bought only when and where needed. Try to find others whose own money machines are up and working and use them to do the things you can't handle yourself. Always force yourself to ask if the service or effort is really needed at all.

An associate approach can also solve the employee problem. If whoever you are living with digs bookkeeping and accounting better than working for a living, split up the project with each of you doing the parts that seem most suited to you. Or, if you are into two separate money machines, each do part of what the other hates worst. Or work with a loosely knit group of other artisans on a cooperative or group basis.

Employer/employee relations also bring on a whole new master-slave trip and the need to funnel time and effort in directions away from your main goal of adding as much personal value as possible to your money machine. When and wherever possible, go on to use the services and money machines of others. Stay away from all boss-worker hassles.

strategy secret—front money will be blown

Having enough advance financing for your money machine is about the **worst** possible thing you can do and is almost certain to scuttle the whole machine.

A glib but accurate reason is that if you have the money, you are only going to spend it. And spend it on things that are totally unnecessary and in ways that will commit you down the road to even higher future costs.

For your money machine to work, you have to start out scared, lean, and hungry. Such frivolities as food, clothing, and shelter should be totally forgotten in getting your money machine started.*

There are lots of good reasons for studiously avoiding excess money when you start your money machine. It's real difficult for any beginner to increase the amount of money he is handling by more than 20% or so a year without starting to do stupid things with it or worrying too much about it.

Money machines expand fastest and best when they bootstrap and pyramid their own output on their own terms. At any time, the materials, plant, and processes you use should reflect the present or known near-future market for what you are doing. Before going to any volume process, always hand-build first dozens, then hundreds of items to make sure they sell and are properly shaken down.

Using other people's money is equally bad. You might feel bad if you've spent it all and have nothing to show for it. This is what usually happens to other people's money. Worse yet, the other people may expect some sort of a return on the cash they put up, and might even think you are obligated to them someway. Your fledgling money machine has enough startup troubles without people like these making things worse.

Of course, some money is needed to start just about anything. But the key is to keep a sense of scale and to start out as simply and cheaply as possible. If a fancy piece of equipment is absolutely essential to do anything at all, borrow one, lease one, or rent one. Maybe buy an old used one that you are sure works. The key rule is to never buy a tool or machine till you are absolutely certain that your present way of doing things is costing you *much* more money than the tool will return. Never buy anything that won't pay for itself in three months. If it can't do it in three months, it's never gonna do it.

One of the saddest (actually the funniest) money machine disasters I've personally seen is the saga of the Escarpment Engineering Corporation. It all started one fine day when a really sharp industrial engineer came up with an improved fire sprinkler. It was a bit out of his field, but it was a mechanically beautiful device. No way did he look into the total market and the way it was head-on competitive with several biggies with a well established distribution. Anyway, he did have a chance—if he had built up a few of these on his own and test sold them. From there he could have bootstrapped his production to match what he was reasonably sure to sell.

---

*but, no matter what, don't let anything interfere with your next hang gliding or caving trip.

Instead, he rounded up a dozen other engineers (no salesmen, accountants, or people—just engineers). Together, this mob came up with ten grand and formed a Sub-S corporation. Now, it turned out they needed *three* fairly accurate holes drilled in one of the working models, so the first thing they did with the ten grand was run out and buy a horizontal boring mill. If the holes had to be that accurate, they should have been eliminated from the design. If they were in fact needed, a local machine shop could have done the job for a few dollars. Then, they took the rest of the money and bought some horrendously expensive injection molds for the sprinkler bodies. In fact, these molds were so fancy, the plastic company even used them in its own ads to show the mind-blowing things that could be done with this particular plastic.

Later field tests, of course, pointed out several major defects in the system, and lots of heavy changes had to be made. No allowance was made for these having to be sold by middlemen, so the final retail price was unreasonably high, pricing the beast right out of the market. Finally, the other engineers got hacked off at the first one and threw him out of his own company.

The really sad thing is that this was a workable product that could have gone on to bigger and better things—but the poor money machine got drowned in a sea of cash and incompetent advice before it ever had a chance to get going.

Some money machines may be capital intensive, needing a lot of machinery to provide an output. Printing presses especially have a way of gobbling up nickels at an incredible rate. Once you buy one, the press is always too small, has maintenance problems, or a special job comes up and makes you run out and buy a better one. Even here, the key is to keep a sense of scale. Use equipment on the cheapest available basis. This is probably purchase-rental on a press since old presses guarantee bad vibes. You should always gear the size of what you need to your expected near-term return.

If it looks like lots and lots of front money cash is the only way to go, scrap your whole money machine and pick a new one. Even when it is up and running perfectly, your money machine *at its largest* shouldn't have more than a year's income tied up in your *total* plant and equipment. This one year limit has been called the *convivial workplace* and forms the dividing line between the good guy or gal craftspersons and the bad guy industrialists.

The really big reason for avoiding front money is that the interest on it forms a fixed expense that, come hell or high water, has to be paid for out of current money machine sales. Ever having *any* fixed obligation is bad, and much more so if you saddle your beginning money machine with heavy obligations like this well into the future. This is one of the reasons that solar energy is having problems getting off the ground. The interest on the money needed to build the system is so high that having free fuel doesn't make much difference. Don't let your money machine get in the same bind.

strategy secret—cash flow is everything

There are lots of possible accounting methods, but there is only one that you should use when starting your money machine and that is simple cash flow.

In cash flow accounting, you keep track of how much money comes into your machine and how much goes out, just like a piggy bank. You enter each and every transaction as it happens in some simple way, like writing it on a "cash out" pad. Once a week you do a running balance of your totals. Once a month, you look at your bottom line to see if you are winning or losing. After several months go by, you project your annual returns.

You don't count anything for materials unused but on hand, things produced but not sold, the value of the place where you work, or things you have delivered but have not been paid for. This sort of accrual accounting can be important for a large corporation, but will only deceive you if you include these things too early in the game. You should set aside income as it comes up for tax obligations, retirement funds, and other fixed expenses that will be paid out at a later date.

A very important rule is to keep your bookkeeping methods very simple but accurate and up to date at all times. Never let them get behind.

While having only enough income to continue your technical or craft trip may be one of the keys to your money machine, it in no way means that you shouldn't pay lots of very close attention to all the cash flow involved. This is one particular place where craftspersons screw up badly. The reasoning is that since they aren't in anything for the money, that money doesn't matter. The great irony in this is that the *less* you are in something for the money, the *more* crucial it becomes to keep track of each and every expense and then to minimize them.

strategy secret—accept no less than a 200% annual return on cash flow

We've already seen how you have to maximize your personal value added for a successful money machine, and how you have to minimize cash and front end expenses along with any fixed obligations. One sure test of whether your personal value added is high enough is whether your income far exceeds your costs. For a viable money machine, you should accept no less than a 200-percent annual return on cash flow.

For instance, in a given year, if you have a total of three thousand dollars in expenses, it should be offset by at least nine thousand dollars worth of income. This leaves you with two nickels generated for every old nickel put up and returned.

Now, a 200-percent annual return on an "investment" seems like an impossible dream to traditional financial people. These days, those kind of people are hard pressed to find a long-term investment that breaks even, let alone gains anything in the face of inflation and taxes.

But we aren't talking about anything traditional or big business. We're talking about your secret money machine that's driven by a few nickels and lots of your personal value added energy. On top of this, the 200-percent annually doesn't have to be tied to a single sale. A monthly sales return of 20 percent, or a daily return of one percent per day is just as good, provided you consistently do this day in and day out throughout the year.

The 200-percent goal means that far fewer dollars have to change hands to keep you in nickels. For instance, if you wanted an income of $20,000 per year, for a 200-percent return on your nickels put in, you can do this with only $30,000 in gross money machine sales. Many traditional businesses, with their multiple employees, high fixed capital costs, limited value added, and intrinsic communications barriers can only show a 10-percent return. In fact, lots of them would be delighted with a 10-percent return. For the same $20,000 income, this means the total gross sales have to be $200,000 when these inefficiencies are thrown in, a value almost seven times higher.

strategy secrets—give them something extra. . .

This secret combines the reason behind the baker's dozen with an old show business maxim. "Something extra" is something added and unexpected that your customer gets over and above what he has paid for.

Some examples:

* Enough premium yarn for a first project with a loom kit

* Giving an editor extra artwork in an attractive folder

* Adding complete documentation to computer software

* Providing sockets and test points on an electronic kit

* Including a plant with a macramé hanging
* Politely answering dumb questions at a crafts fair
* Taking book readers beyond what they expect

One of the greatest something extras of all times has to be that plastic nut starter that *Heathkit* puts in most electronic kits. The thing couldn't possibly cost more than a nickel, but it dramatically simplifies mounting hardware and parts. At the same time, it says that *Heath* cares about the problems you may be having putting things together.

They since have added a piece of bent metal to some kits that lets you remove integrated circuits safely. This is even lower in cost and handier still.

Your something extra should simply say, "Thank you. I care." Whatever it is, it shouldn't be expensive but must be unexpected. If you can't think of anything else, tie a ribbon around your product on the way out the door.

strategy secret— go for it. NOW!

So much good stuff in the way of money machines is passed up because you are afraid to act, afraid to jump, afraid of what others think, or simply assume that there is a big and organized "they" out there whose only purpose in life is to laugh at you or hassle you. *There is no THEY.*

Be assertive. The best way to get something is to ask for it. The best way to stop something is to say no to it. The best way to influence others is to simply tell them how you feel.

. . . and leave them wanting more

The concept of "leave them wanting more" will vary greatly with the particular money machine. In a book or article, you stop when you have reasonably informed, rather than burying the reader in tedium or detail. This tells the reader that you respect his time and commitment to what you have to say. In a craft sale, you set your price and your transaction in such a way that the customer wants to come back. In a rap session, you shut up before you have overstated your case. And, of course, in a live performance, you stop the encores long before the audience stops clapping.

Ideally, you should leave your clients so that as soon as they get word that your new book is out or that your new silversmithing class is open, or that your going to be exhibiting at some fair, they will run out and enthusiastically flock to your money machine.

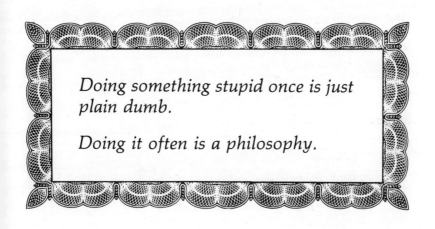

Doing something stupid once is just plain dumb.

Doing it often is a philosophy.

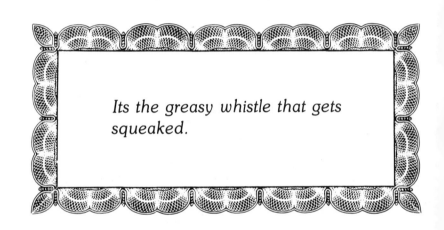

Its the greasy whistle that gets squeaked.

TWO

Secrets II – Tactics

Let's turn now from the big picture to the everyday nitty gritty details of getting your money machine working. One tactic by itself may or may not break you. But the more you use them, the more powerful the base you can build on.

tactics secret—know the difference between cold cash, j-dollars, and megabucks

Cold cash is what you get when you supply a quality product to a known bunch of customers at a bargain price. It is the *only* type of income your money machine should seek.

The letter "j" is the engineer's symbol for an imaginary number. j-dollars are imaginary dollars that simply do not exist. So many starting money machines end up chasing these ephemeral j-dollars and end up with nothing to show for it.

One j-dollar chase starts when you assume some need exists when it really doesn't. It's easy to spend lots of time and effort only to find out that the supposed market couldn't care less about what you have to offer. Some older electronic will-o-the-wisps include specialized timers for sports car rallys, ballistic chronometers, photographic shutter testers, and just about anything else electronic that "should" be useful in the photo market. There's lots of other examples. Usually, you get into the situation where the people whom you think are your market either don't have the money, do the job otherwise, don't believe you, or are smart enough that they don't need your help.

If you are into something very specific and specialized, make sure there's enough nickels available to feed you.

Another j-dollar snipe hunt takes place when you assume something about a market that simply isn't so. A quick quiz:

There is a vast small business computer market that will be much more profitable than the cost-sensitive hobby computer market.

☐ True   ☐ False

Absolutely and totally false. Yes, there probably is a small business computer market. But, subtract out the businessmen who will only deal with name-brand biggies, and old-line management who will only go into computers on a kicking and screaming basis. Include the need for a strong sales force, software expertise, and a well-established maintenance service. Add your image and advertising costs. Allow for the fact that your users will be totally unsophisticated epsilon minuses who won't even look for the on-off switch if the thing seems broken. And throw away completely the hobby computerist who is both knowledgeable and highly motivated. What do you have left?

Not a vast and profitable new market, but one with its own set of severe problems. Not the least of which is that everyone assumes the opposite, so you'll have lots of competitors losing their shirts along with you.

A key rule is to sample a new sales area for your money machine so you are sure that the nickels are there. And if things seem rough in the field you are in, don't ever assume that the problems will magically solve themselves just by your blindly jumping into something else.

Mislocating your market is another good way to go chasing after those wonderful j-dollars. Your products have to be available to people who want or need them. Anyone else couldn't care less.

I know a ceramics type whose pottery is extremely well done, original, sensitive, and shows incredible future potential. But, she lives in a blue collar type of town where discretionary income is largely unknown, as is just about anything in the way of artistic taste or appreciation of fine arts. Besides, she's a hippy and they're all rednecks. As a result, things simply aren't selling and her money machine is having a rough time of it.

Now, it turns out that this particular town is in a very unusual location. If she would look in *any* direction of the compass, she would find a mind-blowing market only a short drive away.

To the south is a town set in one of the most scenic locations in the west. It pulls tourists from all over the country and photographers from everywhere in the world. It has a very lively fine arts trade. To the east is an old mining community that has turned into an artists colony that includes co-op artisan lofts. To the north is an experimental architectural complex that's often used for rock concerts, fairs, craft demonstrations, alternate lifestyle conferences, and so on. And to the west is one of the larger cities in the state with its museums, craft stores, mall shows, street fairs, and university community shops.

As our strategy secret of the last chapter told us, put nothing between you and your customers. Especially a short drive.

One more super way to chase j-dollars is to assume people will buy or do what is good for them. Organic food may be nice, but if it's going to sell or be popular, it has to taste good and be attractively packaged. Bicycling may be great, but if the neighbors are going to laugh and if cars are going to attack you continuously, no way. Same for public transportation. Solar cookers may be where it's at, but no way will they sell until they get cheaper and more fun to use than a barbecue grill. Cost calculators for use in supermarkets will *never* sell, because people who are smart enough to worry about food costs won't go to a supermarket in the first place. They'll be in a co-op or buying wholesale instead.

Now, if you feel as I do that these things are important, fine. But, you'll never sell them by shoving them down somebody's throat. Your product has to fill a need in your customers. And, if the need isn't there, or if you can't help it along with communications or information, you're chasing j-dollars.

Megabucks are those big pie-in-the sky lightning bolts that make you instantly filthy rich beyond your wildest dreams. You do this by taking your new carburetor idea and selling it to Detroit . . . or suing IBM and then collecting for their infringing your computer patent . . . or having an instant best seller once you get your book written and then have to beat the publishers away with a stick . . . or that big "whiplash" insurance settlement.

Well, the unvarnished truth of megabucks is that you will get shellacked every time you go after them. Swampfelder's rules tell us all we need to know:

In any megabuck situation . . .

* The odds of you ever getting one red cent are invariably much lower than you think.

* If the megabucks are ever gotten, they will be received far later than expected and in a non-useful way.

* The final amount, if any, will be miniscule and further reduced by third party ripoffs such as taxes, commissions, attorney fees, and so on.

* In the final accounting, you will always *lose* money.

* Any megabucks you prespend will magnify out of all proportion and become an embarrassment to you.

* The psychic energy blown in pursuing megabucks will always exceed their value by not less than a factor of ten.

So, is there no hope for megabucks at all? It turns out that your money machine has one very real, very simple, and very sure route to megabucks that avoids all of Swampfelder's rules. And this is done by always concentrating your money machine on cold cash transactions. When you see a j-dollar or a megabuck heading your way, either duck, laugh at it, or run the other way.

tactics secret—separate frugality from stupidity

It should go without saying that your starting money machine should do almost everything as cheaply as possible and in a low energy and low profile way. For instance, buying brand-new metal filing cabinets for your starting money machine isn't even stupid. Use orange crates, if you can possibly afford them. If not, find some cheaper substitute, or better yet, get rid of whatever it was you wanted to keep there in the first place.

For practically everything in your new money machine,

* Think simple

* Think cheap

* Think scungy

* Think low energy

* Think small

But, there's at least two exceptions to doing everything as cheaply and simply as possible.

The first, of course, is that anything that goes out the door should show high quality and personal concern. If you are a beginning author, using newsprint on both sides for your rough copy and intermediates is fine and a good idea. But the final, out-the-door copy should be the best quality bond paper you can reasonably get, typed on by a new carbon ribbon. The idea here is to separate what is important from what is not. You then use the most reasonable quality for your final products that you possibly can.

Our second exception applies to a very few of the key tools you use in your money machine. Is a correcting *Selectric* really better than a *Brother* portable? Is a *Nikon* better than an *Instamatic*? Is a *Tektronix* scope better than an *Eico*? You better believe it.

One or two of your key money machine tools should be the finest quality you can get, and more than good enough to do the best work you possibly can. Pride of workmanship is one big reason, as is your ability to put a better product out easier. Just the right vibes that a good tool gives you is enough to change your whole outlook on your money machine and its products.

So, think scungy, except for a few key tools. Make those first rate.

Some common sense is still called for even when you are getting the best possible tools. The tool has to be painfully needed. Whatever you are using now must be costing you energy and money so badly that the new tool cries to be used. The new tool has to pay for itself in three months or less. And, of course, keep your cash outlay as tiny as you can. Now, really bad or really old used tools should be avoided, especially in electronics. Quality rebuilt and guaranteed items are another matter entirely and often a good route. Leasing is another way, as is purchase-rental. Simply borrowing equipment or renting time on somebody else's tools can also solve the problem for you.

Another rule is to never buy something brand new at the list price unless (1) all else has failed, and (2) you will immediately lose a lot of money, energy, and customers if you don't do so.

tactics secret—identify your blind spots

Everybody has something they are really into. But, for everything you are really good at, there's bound to be other things that you simply ignore or don't think are important. An engineer may be an excellent designer but totally turned off by the give-and-take of politics or unable to stomach the dealing and manipulating of people that is involved. A politician can't understand a no-compromise situation or initiating something unpopular or unprofitable when it is needed instead of long after the need has gone. Some scholarly types may be outstanding at classifying, dissecting, and compiling things, but are totally unable to talk plainly, make any value judgment, or see the big picture at all.

All of these things are blind spots. They will very badly hurt your money machine unless you carefully pin them all down.

There's the case of a manufacturer who personally doesn't like to write. He does have a brother-in-law who used to sell printing equipment, so he set up the most enormous in-house printing facility you could imagine. And my, does he grind out paper. Tons of it.

But, his maintenance and repair manuals are the most confusing and the most poorly written in his industry. His data sheets and ad copy are preposterous, grossly misleading, and artistically atrocious.

His proofreading is so wonderful that even *prices* have gone out the door misspelled.

Another individual simply doesn't care much for numbers, particularly those on the account books. As a result, he often forgets to bill people till much later, sometimes undercharges for what his work is worth, and, in general, cuts into his own profits. He is probably also paying far too much in the way of taxes.

The whole thing here is to recognize both what you are very good and very bad at. Find your blind spots and then do something about them.

Once you find your blind spots, recognize that you probably won't ever really correct or eliminate them. To do this makes you into somebody else. Instead, either arrange your money machine to accept and live with the blind spots, or else have someone else whose bag is your blind spot bail you out.

If you don't like to deal with people, become a writer and work long distance through the mail. If one-on-one rapping is your trip, do as much teaching as you can. If you hate numbers, get someone else to help you with them. If you hate to write, get someone else to care about the communications needs of your money machine.

Ideally, your money machine should need as little of your blind spot as possible. If this doesn't turn out to be the case, reset to zero and start over with something more suitable.

tactics secret — beware the granfalloon, my son

A *granfalloon* is any large bureaucratic figment of people's imagination. For instance, there's really no such thing as the Feds or the General Veeblefeltzer Corporation. There are a bunch of people out there that relate to each other, and there's some structures, and some paper. In fact, there's lots and lots of paper. The people sit in the structures and pass paper back and forth to each other and charge you to do so.

All these people, structures, and paper are real. But, nowhere can you point to the larger concept of "government" or "corporation" and say, "There it is, kiddies!" The monolithic, big "they" is all in your mind.

So, what do granfalloons have to do with money machines? Just this. Every time you deal with one, you will get taken. There is no big "they." Only individual people. And if the individual who is promising you things doesn't have a strong and total influence on the individual with the big bag of nickels, you're in deep trouble.

In everyday terms, this means to sell your product to people, not to corporations or government. People make their own purchasing decisions. They stand by them. They're usually highly motivated when they do so and they carry their own wallet in their back pocket. If you ever sell to a company or other organization having more than fifteen people, chances are that there is enough squabbling and in-fighting that the person who is buying may not be in control of the person with the nickels.

An author I once knew was called clear across the country to do some writing for a schlock semiconductor house that was going to hit it big with a new beast called a "microprocessor." Since nobody in their publications division ever heard of these, they wanted someone to bail them out and put together some basic information for them. All for cash-type money, of course.

The author even got a royal tour, accidently being let into the secret mountain laboratory and even saw the reign of terror that the poor designers and technicians were living under.

The author was kept waiting for three days for a magic meeting that was supposed to be a mere formality. The meeting was to take place between the publications division, the technical information people (a vastly different crew from a different plant), and the honchos behind the microprocessor. Well, the meeting eventually took place. At which time one honcho said that the program was secret and no outside help could be used. Which ended that. Except for one very hacked off writer. And one unpaid one.

This was the classic granfalloon squeeze play. Here we have one person, thinking he is the granfalloon, doing one thing, while another one does the exact opposite. Both to the detriment of the granfalloon as well as the money machine involved.

Deal with the people, not granfalloons.

tactics secrets—use the black widow effect . . .

A black widow spider usually spins a web and waits for the next meal to drop by. No way does she go out and try to sell her next meal into coming over for canasta. The same basic idea is a good tactic for your money machine. Whenever and wherever possible, let people come to you and seek you out, rather than vice versa.

This is hard to do, especially if nobody knows you are around. But, if a person seeks you out, he has made an ego decision that he will defend. Should he buy from you, he will defend this decision, even if what he bought doesn't meet his needs. No way will he ever admit he got taken.

Oppositely, if a person feels he was "sold" something, he will easily find minor and even unreasonable faults with it to vent his displeasure.

A customer that comes to you is intrinsically a happier one than one you chase after.

. . . and the "SE" technique

The "SE" stands for *Suppress Ego*. This is a good rule anytime you are one-on-one rapping with anybody, particularly a potential or real nickel source. Let the other person's ego trip bounce off you and show empathy to it, regardless of how misguided or obnoxious it seems. But, if the vibes get too heavy, only put up with as much of this as is consistent with the potential nickel return, and no more.

To use the old Dale Carnegisms—be a good listener and take a genuine interest in others at all times. It's old and shopworn advice—but it works.

Rather than trying to sell something, spend the energy enlarging and strengthening your web.

tactics secret—avoid psychic energy sinks

A *psychic energy sink* is any continuing source of bad vibes that makes you mad enough or involved enough to funnel energy and time away from your money machine. Obvious examples are divorces, anything and everything political, bars, lawyers, and, of course, television.

But, psychic energy sinks come in many forms and guises. A neighbor who insists on flooding you out when he irrigates with ten times the water a sane individual would use is a rather obvious psychic energy sink. A computer that thinks you owe it $17.22 when you don't can either be lots of fun or a real hassle, depending on your own attitude.

Some things are beneficial or innocuous in very small doses but fast become psychic energy sinks if they take up too much time or if they involve you with politics or bad vibes. Establishment stuff like the PTA, scouts, organized local sports, and other church and community organizations are good examples.

Your family can become an utterly bottomless psychic energy sink if your parents or relatives live too close to you. A good rule that is essential for money machine survival is to keep all relatives far enough away that it takes a conscious and determined effort for them to visit you.

Another sad money machine disaster was the case of Bill Benson, who was completely done in by psychic energy sinks.

Bill was a superb photographer, specializing in action-in-motion photographs of destruction derbies, swamp buggy races, soccer matches, and so on. He combined this with a studio, darkroom rentals, a beginner's instruction course, and a very attractive but not-too-bright female assistant. He made use of a white elephant building that was perfect for photo use but a financial disaster to earlier renters because of its location and weird shape.

Bill obeyed most of the strategies and tactics that make for a good money machine. His invention of putting all his exhibit photos on a velcro backing and using a main exhibit cloth on the side of a van made for quick setup and quick sales in the field. His mobile color processing lab was equally a masterpiece. Oh, there were a few rough edges here and there. Like a misconception of what is workable in the way of direct mail, going way overboard on stationary, having no real cost controls, and using a telephone system that was more suited to a small town than a two-room building. But outside of a few rough spots, the act was together and working.

Enter psychic energy sinks stage left and stage right. Not one but two wives, one after alimony, the other after some medical malpractice megabucks. Enter two earlier business entanglements involving someone else's bankruptcy and wrongly seizing some of Bill's working equipment. And exit a source of j-dollars that never materialized. The whole money machine collapsed in a heap of rubble. Bill vanished from the midwest town he lived in and hasn't been seen there since.

Always recognize psychic energy sinks for what they are—sopperuppers of time, energy, and crucial vibes that should go to your money machine. Avoid them at all costs.

tactics secret—let others pay you for your fun

As much as you can, let everything you do have a second purpose of generating extra nickels, or at least saving some of them for you. There's many sources of supplemental income that can go with a particular money machine and its supporting lifestyle. Pick up as many of these as you can and use them as a buffer on your income or else to add to the depth and enjoyment of what you do.

Don't think of these as second income, but as ninth through forty-third sources of income. A few random examples:

* being a part time fireman
* substitute teaching
* giving income tax advice
* doing a regional column for a paper

* growing specialty herbs
* offering a junior college course
* entering contests and competitions
* restoring old pianos
* doing free lance photography
* auctioneering
* critiquing textbooks
* being in a rock band
* helping with a co-op food store
* custom woodworking

The list can go on forever. Check the back issues of *The Mother Earth News* for several thousand more things to do that both generate nickels and are fun and interesting.

The only limit to these is that they should be consistent with what you really want to do and should pay enough (either nickels or psychic energy) to be worth the time and effort you devote to them.

An even better trick is to have others pay you for what would normally cost you a bundle. How much would a nice summer cottage in the woods for a few months set you back? Be in the right place at the right time and the Forest Service, the Park Service, or a State Forester will give you one free and pay you to stay in it as well. As sweeteners, they might even throw in a few B-17 slurry bombers and a helicopter or two for you to play with.

Like to travel? Do stories or photos on where you go and let books, magazines, and papers pay at least part of your way. Want to take a tropic cruise? Do it as part of a scientific expedition and maybe even get paid for it. At the very least, the total expense of the trip can often be tax deductible if the whole deal is for some valid scientific purpose.

You get the general idea. Now, these sound like pie-in-the-sky ripoffs. And they are. But, I've done lots of them. And, if you carefully tune yourself into the "let others pay you for your fun" idea, you'd be surprised how many of them you can pick up and use.

tactics secret—believe in biorhythms

Everything you do is tied into energy cycles in your life. There's a physical energy cycle, a sexual cycle, and a creativity or intellectual cycle. There is some controversy over just how long these multi-week cycles last and whether they are traceable back in time to some long ago event. But, there is little doubt that the cycles presently exist and exist strongly in most people.

You should attempt to predict your current cycles and then force yourself and your money machine to maximize them, rather than continuously fighting them. If you are too tired to work, forget it. You will only botch things up anyway. If everything goes wrong, take the day off and go hide. Why force yourself to write, say, ten pages a day on a book, when the writing will be dull and uninspired half the time and not use enough of your creative energy the other half?

Instead, do extra effort on energy high days. Do extra creative work on intellectual high days and so on.

There's lots of biorhythm books out. Pick one and see if it works for you. You'll have the best results with methods that force you to plot your *present* moods over time, rather than using a method that arbitrarily goes way back in time.

One simple method of keeping track of your creative cycle that probably will work for you is your dreams. First, subtract out the CAP factor*, and then plot those nights you don't dream, those you dream and can't remember, and those nights in which you dream and can clearly remember. A cluster of clearly remembered nights should be closest to a creative high, while no-dream nights are closest to a creative low. Once you have one cycle reasonably well plotted, you should be able to predict the next one and then schedule yourself accordingly.

tactics secrets—some mini-tactics

There's bunches and bunches of mini-tactics that can work for you and your money machine. Here's a large handful for you:

* **Iffen it ain't broke, don't fix it**—Concentrate your efforts on things that need solved and finished, rather than improving or changing things already done.

* **Iffen it ain't cooked, don't serve it**—Never advertise or accept payment or orders for an undeveloped or undeliverable product, no matter how good it's going to be.

* **Always look for the obvious**—The simplest possible explanation and the simplest possible way of doing things is almost always the best place to start.

---

*Coconut Anchovy Pizza

* **Always expect the exact opposite**—When people tell you things, always assume that the exact opposite is a distinct possibility and hedge yourself accordingly.

* **Use out-the-door regimentation**—An undelivered product is a total waste. It's not creative unless it sells. Funnel your psychic energy into getting things done and delivered.

* **Deal direct**—Always handle everything at the highest possible level in the most straightforward possible manner. Avoid ever dealing with secretaries, salesmen, middlemen, agents or manufacturer's representatives.

* **Try a football strategy**—To get into a new product area, first try battering through the middle. Then try an end-around pitch out. Next, a long pass. And if everything fails, punt.

* **Change while you are winning**—The best time to change to bigger and better things is while you are on top, not after disaster has struck. The surest sign to be into better things is when things couldn't possibly be better.

* **Never directly confront big business on their own terms**—They will squash you like a bug. Use a triple reverse instead, leading with what they can't touch—your personal value added.

* **Ease, do not jump, into deep water**—Always explore some new area in the simplest, cheapest, and most minimum way. Watch out for sharks and U-boats.

* **Fine tune your bullshit filter**—Eighty percent of what most people tell you, and one-hundred-fifty percent of what a salesman or politican tells you will be what the Houyhnhnms politely termed "that which is not so." Act and respond accordingly.

* **Profit from the mistakes of others**—Every field has its equivalents to the electronics industry *Viatron, Megastore, Datasync, Ragan, and Ovionics*. Study the big losers and learn from them.

* **Better wrong now than right later**—On any new design, the first attempt *will* have to be done over anyway. So kluge up something *now* and let it teach you the right way to go.

* **Swim, cave, run, fly, drive, cycle, climb, jog**—Or anything else both athletic and non-competitive. Stay in shape. Get dirty. Exhaust yourself. Take a chance.

* **Separate the "yeahbuts" from the "gotcha's"**—A Gotcha is some fundamental reason something won't work, or the crux of the problem to be solved. A Yeahbut is some excuse somebody else

thinks up for why something won't work or isn't practical. Attack the Gotcha's. Ignore the Yeahbuts.

* **Keep a low profile**—Seek a quiet middle ground. Avoid bragging or promises of any type. Keep your plans to yourself, but avoid the extreme of paranoid secrecy.

* **Think, act, and live synergetically**—The whole does not equal the sum of its parts. It's bigger and behaves totally differently. Always force any task to have as many different uses and purposes as possible. Always work toward the big picture.

* **People will always do the exact opposite of what you tell them**—Unless you allow for this ahead of time, in which case they will do as they damn well please.

* **Shut up after the sale**—Anything you say after a purchase decision is made will hurt you. The less said, the better. Don't snatch defeat from the jaws of victory.

* **Psychic energy must be funneled**—You have only so much time and energy, so put it all into your money machine and the things you believe in. Don't let others steal your time and energy.

* **Study the works of chairman Mao**—Know your enemy. Find out everything you can about possible antagonists, detractors, or competitors of any form. Anticipate what they are going to do and then completely change the rules of the game to something they simply won't understand.

* **Avoid sources of poison and bilge**—Get into a funky and liveable environment. Walk away from hassle or bad vibes.

* **Attack the flank, not the front**—This not only works on forest fires, but is good in any high energy field. Similarly, you'll find more fish in quiet backwaters than in a main stream. But stay out of the swamp.

* **Have a place to hide**—It can be a house down the street, a cave, or simply a shell you can crawl into. But, when you need it—use it, and do so often.

* **Never assume institutions or people will change with time**—They won't. Incompetence and greed are immutable physical constants of the known universe.

* **Don't go against the grain of cultural acceptability**—Keep your products in reasonable taste. Don't gross people out.* And

---

*Freak out, yes. Gross out, no.

don't expect them to learn a new typing keyboard or to drive with levers instead of a wheel, and so on. No way will they.

* **Practice Kettering's intelligent ignorance**—Know what it is that you *don't* know about your products and your money machine. Always seek to minimize your own stupidity.

* **Minimize your ripoff potential**—Don't accumulate fancy things with high quick cash value. Make what you have look scungy. Practice reasonable security. Don't set your money machine up to where someone can steal it or use it against you.

* **Play in the cracks instead of on the white keys or the black ones**—Take a different or unexpected approach to any problem. Make your own rules. You are, by definition, the center of the universe.

* **Have sane business hours**—The only insane business hours are 8-5 Monday through Friday. If you are a night person, work at night. If you like watching the chickens get up, have at it. Burst mode or slow and steady. Whatever works, use it.

* **Be hardnosed to freeloaders**—If someone is using up more of your time, energy, or money than you'd like, tell them to shove off, walk away, ridicule them, or give them a dose of incompetence.

* **Screw off a lot**—Go for a bicycle ride. Daydream. Go back to bed. Shoot pool. These are the times when things jell, when problems solve themselves, when new ideas happen.

* **Migrate with the weather and against the crowds**—Go where it's warm in winter and cool in the summer. Hit the hiking trails on Monday nights, the good restaurants on Thursday afternoons. Never stand in line for nothing or nobody.

* **Always give something "free" away**—Full size PC patterns in a kit story is one good example. Anything that looks like a trade secret or something your customer thinks he is getting for nothing will do.

* **Avoid any and all zero sum games**—A zero sum game is something that others have to lose for you to win. Like being one of two barbers in a small town, or doing parity product advertising. Stay away from this bad trip. Pick games where your winning helps others win as well.

* **Thou shall not hassle, unless. . . .** Be a nice guy or nice gal and gentle to others 90 percent of the time. The rest of the time, be either a hardnosed bastard (to prevent your getting ripped off), or

an incompetent moron (to stay out of a bad trip), as your personal needs dictate.

tactics secret—be a doing dogger

A *doing dogger* is someone who makes things happen. Those who act rather than are acted upon. When they are in a cave, doing doggers have to know where the crawlway goes, what lies beyond the siphon, and how far to the next cave over. Doing doggers:

* always get in control of any situation
* never wait in line for anything
* expose themselves to many alternatives
* never waste time unless they really want to
* wonder
* pick a different route home
* read voraciously
* never watch television
* stay away from psychic energy sinks
* do not hassle unless all else has failed
* start things
* stay off the beaten track
* are into their own trip.

Doing doggers have fantastic secret money machines. So can you.

tactics secret—you are your own worst enemy

The most limiting restrictions on your secret money machine are those limits you yourself put on it. It's not the big "they" out there that stops you from accomplishing. It's plain old you. You are your own worst enemy when

* You let others rob you of time and energy
* You fail to set goals

* You don't follow through
* You set your sights too low
* You don't finish what you start
* You get involved in psychic energy sinks
* You don't get products out the door
* You fail to evaluate change
* You don't persist and persevere
* You aren't a doing dogger.

It's not them, it's you. Most "impossible" goals can be met simply by breaking them down into bite size chunks, writing them down, believing them, and then going full speed ahead as if they were routine.

Try it, you'll like it.

THREE

Getting Started

Starting your own incredible secret money machine is easy enough. The real trick is to make it profitable and keep it going once you have started it.

There is only one form of business you should use for your beginning money machine. This is called a simple proprietorship. Which means simply that you own the business. The business is you and you are it. Beyond using a proprietorship, your main startup goals should go along these lines:

* Think simple

* Spend little

* Stay legal

* Avoid future obligations

* Build by bootstrapping

* Maintain a low profile

* Be open to change

* Have a sense of scale

* Keep accurate records

* Know your goals

Let's now check into what's involved in starting up your own machine:

getting started—pick a name

Your money machine has to have a name, and possibly a logo or another image to go with this name. The name first convinces the IRS you really are a business. More on this later. The name gives you credibility to your customers and your suppliers. And, most importantly, the name convinces you that you've really done it.

It's easy to expect a name to do too much for you. A poorly chosen one can easily hurt you, but a good one can only help you to the point you let it. A name should be specific enough that your customer can guess what you are up to. It should be general enough to give you leeway to change your products or even the whole direction of your money machine. A name must be funky. It should give good vibes to your clients or customers in a way they can immediately relate to. A name shouldn't be too cute or too much of an "in" type expression, for it will surely go out of date and become a problem later on.

It's hard to meet all these needs in a name at once since the needs are pretty much opposed to each other. Let's look at some good real-world examples in four different money machine fields:

Weavers have used these . . .

* Rumplestiltskin   * Run of the mill

* Threadmill   * Threadbenders

* Golden Fleece   * The Spider Web

* The Shorn Sheep

while some retail computer stores have picked . . .

* Thinker toys

* Hoboken Computer Works

* Kentucky Fried Computers

* Bit Bucket

* Numbers Racket

* Itty Bitty Machine Company

* Barefoot Computers

and potters have used these . . .

* Earthnfire
* Rare Earth
* Mud Flat
* Dobe Depot

* Bisque Box
* Alaskan Mud Puddle
* Mud in Your Eye

and here's some electronic project names . . .

* Bit Boffer
* The Quiet Mother
* Cheap Video
* Gnu-Matic

* Psyctone
* Quadart
* Spiradoodle

These are all good examples. At least I like them. It's just as easy to come up with bunches of bad ones as well. How's "Nora's Ceramic Shoppe" for a real turn-on?

Negative images are real easy to produce. They can, and will, turn customers off. For instance, there really is an electronic manufacturer with the tradename *Fluke*. There really is a direct mail outfit in Thief River. Using the next post office over has to be better, sight unseen. I actually know a John Smith, and he is a very creative electronics type with several money machines going. But, he used to call himself *John Smith Enterprises*. At least to me, this is a name that cries "RIPOFF" in capital letters. Enterprises-anything is ungood. Almost as bad is . . . "and Associates."

You can also pick a name or an image so close to somebody else's that they will get the credit and you will go unnoticed, especially if they are biggies and you aren't. If you are heavy into electronics, you probably noticed a delightful cartoon type of ad that used to appear in several of the trade journals. The strip starred two characters, a vivacious female, *Anna* and a klutz engineer, *Log*. The strip was funny, very easy to read, and had an unusual "across the bottom" type of ad layout that cried to be read. And it seemed like some of the best advertising that *Analog Devices* ever had.

What made the strip even better for *Analog Devices* is that it didn't cost them one red cent. The cartoon was run by some *other* company whose name I can't remember. Do you?

Avoid getting anything worn out and hackneyed into a name or an image. For instance, there is a miserable type font called

AVANT GARDE

Now, this is a typeface that only a typographer could love. Yet, it gets used over and over again in the most unlikely places. Using the checkbook font to get an

ELECTRONIC IMAGE

is done so often that it, too, is hackneyed, besides being very hard to read.

The word "affordable" is something that drives me up the wall. It started out as a meaningless but "in" expression, but now comes off plain ridiculous. To prove this to yourself, everytime you see the word "affordable," replace it with "lemon scented."

My own company name *(Synergetics)* doesn't meet these guidelines we've looked at very well. But, it does separate the doing doggers (those into Fuller) from the turkeys (those not) and it's a riot listening to establishment-type secretaries and others stumble over it during a phone call. But that particular name is something I very much believe in and is very much a major key to my own money machine.

Your name and your image tend to be self-fulfilling, so be sure to provide for this in your choice. In many money machines, your customers may never see you, particularly if you are into direct mail. Your name, your logo, and your image can be all they ever have to go on.

One important rule is to bounce your new name off some others to see how they react. A sure sign of success is if your friends and relatives think the name is the dumbest thing they ever heard. As long as your customers don't agree, you're all set.

getting   started—register   it

Registering your name makes it legal. It gives you credibility. It keeps anyone else from using the same name, at least locally. Once registered, the name can transact business, receive checks, and so on. Since the cost of registration is low and there is only the usual amount of hassle involved, every money machine should be registered.

Usually, you register your name on the state level. The details will change with your state, but things generally go like this:

There will be a "trade name registery" or "fictitious names act file" kept by the secretary of state or the state commerce department. You go to them and tell them you want to register a name. Then you fill out forms and pay them five or ten dollars or so.

Before they register your name, they might insist that:

* No one else is using the same name
* The name is not obscene
* The name doesn't sound like another
* The name has no obvious ripoff potential
* The name has something to do with
the business to be conducted

Things will be easiest if you actually go to your state capital during midday and midweek and chase things around yourself. But you should be able to do everything by mail and telephone if you are willing to make a few calls to the wrong places.

Some counties or larger cities might also like you to register your business name. This may be a good idea if there's likely to be lots of similar money machines in your particular area. It can be a very bad idea if the name registration person happens to be on speaking terms with the zoning or licensing people. Since I'm probably the only electronic consultant in a county that's larger than most New England states, I personally haven't bothered with a county registration.

Should you have any trouble, check into a library or a university bookstore. They ought to have a copy of something similar to *The Legal Aspects of Doing Business in Arizona* that applies to you. Make sure the book is written for people and not lawyers. The book or booklet should give you the details you need on registration.

Be very suspicious if there seem to be stiff fees involved or legal help is asked for. You will most likely be getting ripped off if this happens. If all else fails, move to a reasonable state.

When your name is registered, they'll send you a fancy certificate suitable for framing. Usually the registration is good for three to five years before you have to renew it.

getting started—get some stationery

Here is one time when middle ground is far and away the best. Even when you are just starting, you probably should have some sort of business stationery. Rubber stamps or stick-ons simply won't hack it, and will look as bad as using a ball point pen on tablet paper torn out of a binder.

On the other hand, it's easy to blow several hundred dollars on custom printing that may not meet your needs, particularly if you change money machines or a working address.

So, get the cheapest decent stationery you can, and just enough of it to handle a few months' worth of activity. You can do this with *semi-custom* letterheads. These are available from lots of direct mail outfits like *New England Business Services* and *Fidelity,* as well as larger office supply stores. Printers tend to be an expensive source for simple, low-cost stationery.

A semi-custom letterhead gives you a choice of four or five background styles and half a dozen type fonts. You pick something close to what you would eventually like to have. The best selection will miss by 1.60935 kilometers, but use it anyhow. Always check three or four places before committing yourself. Others may have something better, cheaper, or both.

Sometimes a large supplier may offer a stock letterhead with an imprint. This can be very cheap if it meets your needs. My first money machine* was called *West Penn Sound* and was into public address system rentals, repairs, and audio design. At the time, *RCA* offered a standard letterhead for TV service shops that was custom imprinted. It was a ways back, but the cost was something like $3 per ream, including envelopes, so I used these. If you can luck into something that is suitable, use it.

Your money machine might call for something other than letterheads. Very personal money machines like painters, potters, stained glass artisans, and so on might want to use quality note paper instead for a better image. Others might want or need business cards. Semi-custom shipping labels may also be called for.

At any rate, your low cost stationery should be just barely enough to get you credibility and only quantity enough to get you started. You can go on to bigger and better things when you are bigger and better.

getting started—go to a bank

Next, go to a bank. But, do NOT talk to them. Do NOT tell them you are in business. Instead, quietly change your checking account to the type of "commercial" service (free checks—minimum balance) that is halfway between a personal and a true business account setup.

Pick a sedate and legitimate looking check style. Have them print both your company name and your name immediately below it with

---

*As Scrooge McDuck would say, "Good old number one."

your address. Avoid the checks with a "Susie Homemaker" image or those with pink saguaro cactuses or green flamingos on them.

Now, and this is the tricky part. Tell the bank you sometimes sign your name differently and, if they haven't given you one already, ask them for an "alternate signature card" or an "alias card" to fill out. Sign the card every possible way you would receive income normally, such as Alvin Snurdley, A. Reginald Snurdley, A.R. Snurdley, Al Snurdley, and so on. Then add your business name to one of the empty blanks. If they ask, mumble something incoherent or say it's part of a hobby.

What you've done is perfectly legal. Any check now made out to your company name is now yours to cash. You simply sign the company name, followed by your own, or else you use a "for deposit only to the account of . . ." stamp and your name. Number your checks starting with No. 4000. A supplier getting your check No. 002 hurts your credibility.

Our whole aim here is to keep a low profile and minimum costs. You've completely avoided the hassles and expense of a formal business account, but are still legal.

You should also back up this checking account with some automatic loan guarantee *Credit Reserve* sort of thing. Get the maximum credit line you possibly can.

But, rule number one is to *never use this credit intentionally.* It is there to protect your business from the bad vibes of a bounced check and to cover arithmetic errors. It also bails you out should you receive some bad paper and not have it clear. Don't even use the credit reserve to cover float. Always keep a positive enough balance in this account such that if all checks were to clear *immediately,* you wouldn't need this safety backup.

getting started—find a place

It's interesting to look around at the winning money machines and see just how many of them got there the hard way. The hard way is to start with an expensive commercial building or something new and custom built. Later on, the money machine backs way off and switches to something simple, liveable, and more suitable. Almost always, the cheap and funky workplace ends up more productive and more profitable. The changeover point usually is the time when the trip into the megabucks really begins.

Starting out at home at first is a good idea. But it is absolutely essential that your workplace is one hundred percent set aside for your money machine. The first reason for this is once again the IRS. As we'll see later, certain business deductions will be disallowed if you don't do this. A second reason is that your workplace forces you into dividing your time between money machine and non-money machine activities, something that's easiest on a "this is where it's at" basis.

A crucial rule is that your workplace must start out as a sacrosanct lair. Very violent and otherwise ungood things should immediately happen to any child, neighbor, or relative who tries to violate this space. Even slow learners must see the light on their first and only trip. People don't drop in on Ford's production line for an idle chat with someone; it's just as important they don't do the same thing to you.

It's often hard for people to realize that you are working when you are obviously home goofing off. This is particularly a problem if you are living in a small town, are a him, and have a her out substitute teaching or something. The only solution to this is to play the role and make yourself look as despicable as you can.

Despite this particular hassle, the best places for money machines are small, independent towns and rural areas, particularly in the mountain west, and away from big cities.

In larger towns and more populated areas, you may find your workplace violating some zoning laws. As long as you aren't running a boiler factory, a sauerkraut works, have thousands of strange looking walk-in customers, or a fifty-foot-high neon sign out front, you can probably get away with some non-blatant zoning violations for a long time. "Ignore but do not confront" is a good policy here, particularly during startup. If zoning turns into a psychic energy sink—move, don't hassle.

Maybe you'd like to work somewhere away from home. Some narrow-minded and inconsiderate apartment owners might get uptight if you put a forge in the kitchen or a kiln on the patio. If you have to separate where you work from where you live, make sure the two are an easy walk or bicycle ride apart. Do NOT ever pick a workplace that takes an automobile ride to get to. Cars used this way are a psychic energy sink and a fixed commitment to a bad scene.

Wherever it is, your monthly workplace costs should never exceed *one percent* of your expected gross sales. Thus, if your starting money machine is only expected to gross $10,000 a year, your maximum rent or payments needed for the workplace must be less than $100 per month. Under no circumstances should you build or buy anything new just for your starting money machine. This is to minimize any fixed future obligations that may become a white elephant to get rid of if you abandon or change your money machine. Eventually, bigger and better places may be called for. But, not till your money machine is off the ground and knows the direction it is taking you in.

No matter where, your workplace must be just that—something with a sense of place. You have to feel you belong there and that it is a part of you. You should be able to fingerpaint it purple, nail up obscene posters, play ELO wall-to-wall, grow exotic plants, work barefoot,

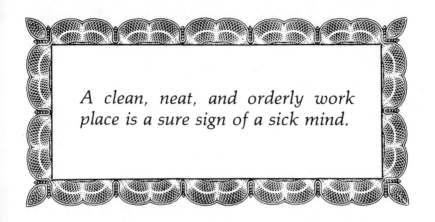

A clean, neat, and orderly work place is a sure sign of a sick mind.

munch magic cookies, drink beer—or whatever—and do any of these with nobody objecting.

Let's look at some real money machine workplaces and see how they are set up, so you can get more ideas on what works.

* **Don**—Alias me. Money machine is electronic consulting, technical writing, and kit design. Started out wrong by building new a custom, architect-designed studio. Later switched to a small house in a smaller town. Most of work now done in one 12 × 20 foot room holding electronics lab, printed-circuit layout area, machine shop, library, and so on. A separate small house down the street is rented for $50 a month and holds the darkroom, loom collection, overflow library, and circuit board processing setup.

* **Max**—Money machine is T-Shirt screening and custom litho camera work. Started out wrong by renting part of large new industrial building. Driven out by dust, high fixed costs, and a timely flood. Bought a distress city lot with three older houses on it. Rents front house out as residence to cover fixed expenses. Second house has accounting area, art layout, stock storage, the huge litho camera (bought for $24!), and a darkroom. The third house holds the screens, ink storage, and a large drying oven.

* **Franny**—Money machine is silversmithing classes and custom jewelry. Initially worked at home and taught classes in a local junior college. Expanded by buying an old, sprawling building whose previous business failures included a laundromat, a used furniture store, and a second-hand trading post. She now offers her evening courses here, has her own work area, and uses this as a home base as she travels to other schools and exhibits.

* **Doug**—Money machine is a direct mail specialty bookstore combined with custom printing and presswork. Started in three small adobe houses in a very low rent district, putting the litho camera and the pasteup in what used to be a pantry. Later moved to a distress building that failed as a french fry crinkling factory.

* **Bill**—Money machine is electronic production aides combined with special motion picture services. Retired from the construction business to do all his work in an old garage. Old garage is a few steps away from one of the finest beaches in the world.

* **Forrest**—Money machine is popular science writing, model rocketry and laser consulting. Writing is done in one bedroom of a trailer. Everything else happens in a 6-foot-square metal shed reminiscent of the corrugated iron one in *Bridge on the River Kwai*. This tiny shed holds a complete darkroom, a bicycle repair shop, an entire optics lab, electronic instruments, a library, product files, model rocketry stock, robotics and solar energy research materials, and heaven knows what else. Very frugal and takes a very meticulous person—but it works and works well.

* **John**—Money machine is electronic music kits, free lance advertising, and retail computer sales. Has an establishment-type factory and lots of employees. His own value added is greatest in new product design. To do this, he bought the house across the street at a super low price and tore out all the inside walls, leaving one very large and very private electronic lab. This in a scenic lakeside setting well away from the factory and its hassles.

* **Earl**—Money machine is custom millwork, loom designs, and replication of very old furniture. Retired from the engineering ratrace as an accomplished designer and author. Enclosed the area beneath the deck of a home on a high, windswept desert. Has woodworking tools in this enclosed area, and uses an expanded bedroom as library, painting, and design areas.

Now, none of these workplaces will take the Chamberettes Outstanding Commercial Improvement Award for the month of February. But, they all work and hold money machines that are far more profitable and more rewarding than the traditional establishment workplaces.

getting started—make a few products and test them

You should test your fledgling money machine on a very small scale before committing yourself heavily. The next startup step is to generate a few quality products and see how they place. Do this with a minimum of future obligations or very heavy time and energy involvement.

For instance, you could make up a dozen pieces of pottery and take them to a trade fair. Or you might try out a course you want to teach at a nearby junior college. Or you might write a travel story or two. Maybe something that right now can be sold as an article, but later will become a book chapter. Perhaps you could print up a few how-to booklets for a direct mail experiment. Or build a couple of solar cookers. Or a hobby computer software system.

Keep the quality of these products your best effort. Make them first rate. The trick is to keep them simple and straightforward enough that even your best effort doesn't take too much time or money. You'll want to avoid expensive tools at this time. Use someone else's kiln, enlarger, oscilloscope, computer, plotter, whatever. If something eventually is going to need fancy assembly tools, hand fabricate a few models the hard way first.

Next, set aside half of your products, leaving only the best ones. Then test sell these somehow, staying as cheap and simple as possible. Use a trade fair or a mall show. Put them in somebody else's store. Use a small ad in a local *White Sheet* or *Pennysaver,* or an even smaller classified in a special interest magazine. Submit a story or two to a carefully chosen publisher. Exhibit at a fair. Do a direct mail project for a magazine. Offer only the key parts (circuit boards, panels, software tapes, etc.) or else keep the project simple and cheap enough that the whole thing can be offered without too heavy an advance commitment.

If your money machine is a winner, you'll know almost immediately by the enthusiastic results you'll get. Now, you probably won't get very many nickels at this stage of the game. But, if the potential for cold cash is there, it should be obvious. Pay particular attention to what sells and how it sells. What you initially think you want to do will usually be different from what your money machine wants you to do best. Adjust things accordingly. Be ready to change and try something else.

getting started—think about your image

If your new money machine looks promising, add a limited additional amount of nickels and effort aimed at making you look larger, more professional, more credible. Add one or two key tools, but keep their cost in line and only have them meet the needs of your money machine for the next few months.

Some of the things to look at now might include:

* **Advertising**—You'll want to expand your web so that the Black Widow effect can work for you. The best advertising is *always* word of mouth from satisfied customers. On top of this, free publicity from product news releases, fair promotion, and so on, can be combined with a limited amount of specific display or classified ads. Always include the price in any ad.

We'll be looking at ads in a bit more detail later.

Many of the obvious places to advertise simply aren't worth the bother. While small, succinct classified ads put in limited circulation, special interest magazines can be useful, the same is generally *not* true of mass-distribution high circulation magazines without a specific audience. Despite the many "Get rich quick with classified ads" rips the usual response to a typical mass market ad is very low and often misdirected away from the people you need as clients. Matters are made worse by the facts that few people bother to read all the classified ads, and that so many scams are associated with this type of ad.

Your foremost ad rule should be to test everything you do on a small scale, and go only with the stuff you know works.

The biggies in classified and direct mail have these rules of thumb—A two percent response to a direct mail campaign is typical—A 5:1 difference between your costs and the selling price is essential, and—a two-step conversion in which you remail to a "free details" ad is also a must. Somehow these rules of survival for this type of advertising seems contrary to what we are out to do with a money machine. Try them, and you are only running dollars around and around at your customer's expense and your psychic energy.

* **Telephone**—Alexander Graham Kernatski's rule states that anything you do with the phone company will cost you three times what you expect. Simply using your home phone can be the best, providing it doesn't swamp out a party line. You can put an extension phone *anywhere,* not just in the same building. It can go down the street or across the country. The cost, of course, goes up with the distance. The phone company usually won't let you use a business listing on a home phone, so if a *Yellow Pages* ad is needed, be sure to include the cost difference between home and business service in your evaluation.

One trick to minimize long distance charges that works out here in the west is to call people at 7:55 AM. You can call across the country for 22 cents or so and hit most people during business hours. The other direction, done at 5:05 also works, but costs more.

You can attach most about anything that won't degrade the phone system these days and not have to buy it from the phone company. These include your own extension phones (leave the ringer out), call directors, dialers, answering machines, computer modems, and others.

Watts lines ("800" numbers) will almost certainly cost you far more than they are worth, besides tying somebody up to handle all the calls. There's two types of service, outward Watts that lets you make all sorts of cheap calls, and inward Watts that let others call you at your expense.

Don't use a phone unless you really need it. If only a few people are going to call you, list the phone in somebody else's name. This is the ultimate unlisted number. If you must use a phone, remember that you are in charge of it and not vice versa. To keep your head in the right place, always ignore every seventh call or at least one call per day.

* **Credit**—Letting people pay you by Bank Americard, Visa, Mastercharge, or something similar is often a good idea. The charges (around 4%) will be more than offset by the number of extra impulse buying sales they generate. You are also protected against bad paper. Talk to your bank for more details. Most credit card outfits are aggressively seeking new places to accept cards.

* **Tax Stamps**—If you are heavy into retail trade, you probably will need a state or city tax number. This frees you from paying sales taxes on some things you buy locally, but you, in turn, have to collect from your customers. The listing also helps your credibility when buying wholesale. On the other hand, there's a lot of hassle, snooping, and paperwork involved. As much as possible, gear your products to things that are tax exempt (written and published things often are), or sell out of state, or sell through others and let them worry about the tax hassles. Be sure to check into the local tax law carefully, and keep a very low profile on any deviations you may make from it. Also check into city business licenses to see if you can avoid getting one without any problems.

* **Post Office**—Tell them your new name and that you will accept mail for it. This covers you if someone forgets to write your name down or gets only a partial address. A post office box is a good idea. It lets you relocate without changing everything. It is more secure. The mail gets beat up less. The address sounds more like a business.

Be sure you know the postage regulations, since some rates (like for books) are much cheaper than others. But, there are specific restrictions you have to meet. Always be super nice to post office people no matter how obnoxious they get. It's extremely important to stay on good terms with them.

A postage machine may be a good idea if you are into mailing lots of oddball things and if an image is important. The meters cost under $10 per month, but are one more of those fixed expenses you should avoid. Usually, you rent the machine from somebody like *Pitney-Bowes* and then take it to the post office where it gets "filled" with $99 worth of postage.

For sending or receiving packages, check into using *United Parcel Service* instead of the post office. They are often cheaper, quicker, and more reliable.

* **Memberships**—If your money machine is heavy into an establishment trip, consider joining the Chamber of Commerce, the Rotary, or things like this. If you're into alternate lifestyles use the Briarpatch, crisis centers, environmental groups, co-ops, and so on. Don't overlook local crafts guilds and clubs, as well as professional organizations. All of these can give you credibility, information, contacts, and, above all, sales. The trick in deciding on any membership is to pick up as much in the way of benefits as you can without getting bogged down in fees, excess time, or loss of psychic energy.

getting started—expand by bootstrapping

By now, your incredible secret money machine should be up and working. The only little remaining problem is that it's still too small to support you, and you may still be putting more money and effort into the money machine than you are getting back. Your next step is to expand the machine by bootstrapping. Generate a lot more products, add a lot more energy, a whole bunch more personal value added, and a little more cash. Increase the scale of your machine gradually and let it continuously feed on itself.

A very important thing to attack now is *efficiency*. Some things you are now doing are taking too long or are blown on things the customer doesn't notice or couldn't care less about. On the other hand, there's some things you *aren't* doing that are super important to your customers. Ask yourself (1) How can you reduce the time and energy that are going into your products? and (2) What are you leaving off that is important?

This lesson was driven home to me way back even before my first real money machine. I was into selling electronic scrap and other things at nearby hamfests, and had picked up free a decent tube tester whose only faults were a broken glass face on the meter and a worn-out socket. I replaced the socket to get the beast working perfectly. But, it wouldn't sell. At any price. People looked at the "open" meter face and assumed that the instrument was a pile of junk. Finally, I glued in a 17-cent piece of plastic to make it look like the meter had a glass face. The tester immediately sold for a then princely $35, the instant it was offered.

Something that wasn't important to me turned out to be the key to a customer's buying. Always watch for this in your own money machine.

At this stage of the game, your money machine will be much smarter than you are. It will almost certainly want to take you in a different direction than you had first planned on going. Listen to your money machine, and listen carefully. So long as the direction the machine is headed is consistent with your *overall* lifestyle goals, follow it. Do not doggedly insist on continuing exactly what you set out to do. Listen and learn from your money machine, and someday you might be as smart as it is now.

Avoid dumping in lots of cash during your bootstrapping. Cash is hard for a money machine to digest and it clogs up the gears. This is especially the case if it is other people's money or something that you have fixed future payments on. Your bootstrapping must concentrate on generating more personal value added, improving efficiency, and getting more things out the door.

Always be alert to change. Be able to adjust and adapt the best match between what you initially set out to do and what your cold cash customers want.

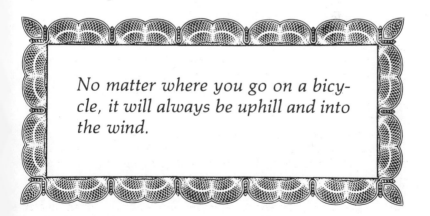

No matter where you go on a bicycle, it will always be uphill and into the wind.

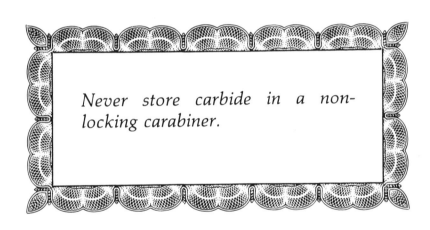

Never store carbide in a non-locking carabiner.

FOUR

Keeping Informed

I subscribe to 137 different magazines. I do this because these are my main source of information flow, and information flow is the key to my money machine.

As we've seen, raw information is the highest energy stuff there is and the easiest to add lots of personal value to. Your best customers will be those who come to you as their main and most reliable source. Even if you don't directly sell information, getting in total control of it will make your products better, customer communications more effective, and your money machine more rewarding.

Our next three chapters are going to be on information flow and how you can control it. This is the "gozinta" chapter on getting, filtering, saving, and controlling information. The next two chapters are the "comesoutta" ones that deal with how to use words and pictures to deliver controlled high-value-added information to yourself and your customers.

keeping informed—tune yourself in

Actually, everything you do involves information flow in some way. The trick is to gather in, filter, and save only the good stuff that will be useful to you. So, step number one is to **think of everything you do in terms of information flow.** Tune yourself in to gathering stuff only from those sources you've found to be useful or feel might be useful to you. Above all, make yourself aware of how and why others are trying to inform you.

Step number two is to **save everything reasonably useful.** So many money machines are complicated by needless stupidities such as

* Forgetting somebody's name
* Losing a telephone number
* Paying too much for something
* Not having the right tax records
* Having to find something over again
* Missing a key detail

Now, how you save things will depend on your particular trip and what works for you. I keep a running series of notebooks that are a cross between a diary, an engineering notebook, and an address log. On top of this, I have some files where I stash useful product information, a reprint file of key articles and technical papers, another file of my own past work, a large library, a small stash for current work, and a business file where every receipt and expense is meticulously kept.

Note the "reasonably" in reasonably useful. It's so easy to let an engineering notebook become a work of art that takes several hours per day, becoming an end in itself. Product files can overwhelm you easily if you save too much too long. And old magazines can gobble up house and home if left to accumulate.

With one exception, you want to make your information saving as *efficient* as you can. Keep only the things you are reasonably sure will be handy to you. Spend only the bare minimum of time and effort in actually filing, writing things, or putting things where they belong. Always do these things *immediately* as you think of them. At least once a year, filter what you've saved and either chuck out anything out of date, or else donate it to a school, a library, or someplace else. If there is a local source of something that's only slightly important to you, don't save your own copy. As with everything else in your money machine, keep a sense of scale.

The one exception is your business receipts and tax records. The rule here is to **save everything forever,** organized as completely and neatly as you can. More on this later.

Tune yourself in. Always make it a habit to look at things and read things, no matter where you are or what you are up to. Keep a way to write things down with you at all times. Watch, look, and listen. Above all, read.

keeping informed — avoid information sinks

Just as there are sources of information, there are also *information sinks*. An information sink sops up information, destroys it, muddies the water around it, or otherwise renders it useless. Information sinks work many ways. They can create an environment where you don't have a chance to think. They can use up your time. They can put you in a passive "acted upon" state instead of an active "doing dogger" state. They can tell you "that which is not so," either intentionally, as part of an ego trip, or through plain stupidity.

Carefully identify and recognize these bad-guy information sinks, and avoid them at all costs. Once you start looking around for them, you'll be surprised at how many there are and how much they compete with each other to rip you off. If you let them, no way will they ever let you pick up anything useful in the way of information.

The worst information sink, of course, is television. It puts you in a passive, comatose state. It spoon feeds you drivel. It is in total control of what it gives you. It makes you expect the instant and certain solution to everything in precisely half an hour. It lacks subtlety, degree, option. It averages you in with the Epsilon minuses. Worst of all, it rents your bod out to the highest bidder, something that the civil war purportedly decided was a no-no.

A newspaper may or may not be an information sink. If you occasionally buy one when you are after something specific like some ads, weather information, financial facts, travel, classifieds, and so on, then your newspaper is a very useful information source. If, on the other hand, you automatically have one delivered each day, meticulously read the advice to the shopworn, the horoscopes, all of the comics instead of just *Doonesbury,* and otherwise blow an hour or more on it, then your newspaper is an information sink of the worst sort. Even believing the news presented or supposing that this is the only thing important that is happening is enough to rob you of useful perspective.

Book clubs are another information sink. They tell you what you are supposed to read. Technical book clubs are super bad in that they often use only one publisher, and push only the out-of-date, poorly written dogs that aren't selling.

Remember that everybody who is presenting you with information is doing so to make a profit. It may be a dollar profit or an ego profit, but it's a profit none the less. Always ask, "Why are you telling me this?" So long as the information source's profit does not come from ripping you off, you're onto a good source.

Look around you today and see if you can't come up with a dozen examples of your own information sinks that are robbing you of useful time and useful knowledge. Some more sinks:

* Anyone who does not read

* Anyone who knows not whereof he speaks

Modifying a television set for a better money machine:

1. Locate the line cord on the set. This is the wire that goes down and plugs into the wall outlet.

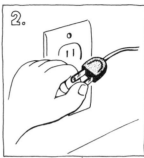

2. Remove the line cord from the wall outlet and hold it by the prongs in your left hand.

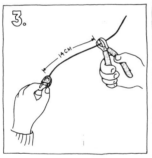

3. Carefully locate a point on the line cord exactly fourteen centimeters from the point where the wire meets the plug. Use a pair of shears or other cutters to cut the line cord in two at this point. Make sure you are still holding the cord by the prongs when you do this.

4. Discard one or both remaining pieces.

* All politicians

* Anyone who does not value time

* Ivory tower types who lost reality

* All salesmen

* Every ad that doesn't show price

* All experts and specialists

* Any source that's overpriced

On your own list of information sinks, be sure to name names and places. Be specific. Identify the enemy. Then ignore, avoid, or ridicule the sink to get it out of your life.

keeping informed—the library is where it's at

I almost managed to get through my senior year in college without ever once having gone near a library. The only reason I went then was a sneaky professor forced it on us by suddenly marching us over there under graduate student guard. After sitting through a boring lecture from a snooty librarian on the card catalog, we finally got out. It was the longest class hour I can remember. It was only well into graduate school that I finally got into libraries and realized how absolutely essential they are to a money machine.

It's a hard lesson to learn, but libraries are where it's at. Find a good one and learn to use it regularly and heavily. It should be your first, best, and cheapest information source.

Now, you do have to pick a good one. For instance, there's a nice new library just down the street. It's a quiet place since nobody ever goes there. And it has lots of books.

For instance, the book they have on their technology shelf. This is a very interesting 1938 text on air conditioning. It's even an *Audel* book—a Sams affiliate. They have very helpful and polite assistants. For instance, I asked one where Bowker's *Books in Print* was and she nicely told me to look it up in the card catalog. It turned out that she was sitting on it since the stool was too short.

You might want to aim your sights a little higher than this. Your best bet will be a main library at a major state university. These libraries are usually open to anyone, although they often discourage children. Most state residents can qualify one way or another for a library card if you want to borrow books on your own. Much of what will be useful to you in a library won't be available for loan anyway, so a card isn't all that important.

63

The *least* useful things in a good library are its books. Most of them will be out of date. The better ones will be on reserve or out on loan. There will often be a bias against technical paperbacks. In an explosive field like electronics or hobby computers, the books they have won't usually be of much help. The only real exceptions to this are when you want to get into some other field and pick up the basics from the best sources. Or, when you need some standard information that doesn't change very fast, such as mathematical tables, standards, shop information, and so on.

So, why on earth would you go to a library if the books aren't going to be helpful to you? Here's some of the things that are important to me:

* **Current Periodicals**—The most useful and current information in an explosive field will be in the magazines. The magazines will be in the library as well, since they usually aren't loaned out for more than an hour or two at a time. A decent library will subscribe to 20,000 or more *different* periodicals, so there's bound to be something in there for you.

  If you are totally new to this trip, start out at the reference desk with something called *Uhrlicht's Periodicals Dictionary,* and use the subject guide to narrow things to a few dozen suitable magazines. Then go to the *Public Serials List* to find what the library has in stock. The list will usually be just outside the counter where you order the magazines and will be a great heaping bunch of computer printout, or else a microfiche reader and a handful of cards. Then sample what's available. Usually you can only get three or so current ones at a time, unless you luck into a library that still has open stack periodicals.

  You'll usually find older periodicals bound into yearly volumes. These are a very good idea mine. It's also interesting to follow these volumes clear back to year zero. This can give you a total perspective of where the field is now, how it got that way, and where it is headed.

  You'll be amazed at the creativity and innovation that early doers in any field have. You might also find some very old ideas that can be easily and profitably updated. A review of things long ago and far away can put present controversy in a totally new light. While you probably won't get emotionally involved in the early 30s *Radio News* controversy of glass-versus-metal vacuum tubes, this issue is an instant replay of the "We're going to shoot you out of the saddle" versus the "No Way" sides of just about any of today's technical innovations.

* **Science Citations Index**—There are reference indexes for just about any field. Typical are the *Readers Guide to Periodical Literature, Chemical Abstracts,* the *Music Index,* and so on. You'll find lots of indexes at the reference desk. While indexes in general are useful and a good starting point, most of them share a common fault—you can only go backwards through time to pick up older and older material.

Would you believe there is an index that lets you move *forward* through time, picking up newer and newer material instead? It's called the *Science Citations Index.* Every time anything is referenced in the bibliography of something newer, it gets listed. Now, every field has its early "horses mouth" source documents. If you are into active filters, its *Sallen and Key.* If you are working with unfocused solar collectors, *Winston* is it. Any competent new material in either of these fields, by definition, *has* to reference these papers.

There's lots of ways to use this backwards index. Since it takes a pretty dumb author to not reference himself every chance he gets*, you can first find out what the original honchos were up to in their later work. The people who first reference the source documents in turn become referenced by yet newer researchers, and so on, generating a list of authors who are active in the field. At the same time, magazines that are heaviest in a field will be referenced most often. This gives you a clue where to go for brand new material.

* **Inter-Library Loan**—All libraries have an Inter-Library loan service, meaning you can borrow anything from anywhere. There are limits to the service to keep it from getting swamped with requests for paperback mystery novels, the response can be slow, and there is some cost involved. You have to look serious and be persistent. You also have to know exactly what you want. But it does work. The only time I happened to need it, the ILL reprint turned out to be in Japanese. But, I did manage to get it translated, and it turned out to be some extremely helpful information.

There's a much more for-sure but expensive route to getting most any reprint from any periodical. It's called

> University Microfilms International
> 300 North Zeeb Road
> Ann Arbor, Michigan, 48106

---

*See, for instance, the *Active Filter Cookbook* (SAMS 21168), or The Lost Wax Mapping Technique, *Cave Crawler's Gazette,* Volume XI, No. 2, p18—19.

and they have just about everything stashed on microfiche. The service is prompt and their stock is mind-boggling.

* **Cheap Xerox**—Around here copy costs are still a quarter a page, take it or leave it. Most libraries will give you a two-page reduced copy for a nickel, either through their own service or on a do-it-yourself machine. Just this 10:1 savings alone more than pays me to make the long trip to the library. Use their machines or service to get information out of non-circulating books and magazines for your own use, as well as a cheap and private way to do lots of your own copy work.

* **Non-Books**—My favorite here is a complete map file of most areas of the country. Most large libraries will also have a film and cassette loan service, a patent file, other federal documents, leaflets, newspapers, special interest materials, phone books, yellow pages, city indexes across the country, and so on. Look around and you'll also find microfiche and microfilm readers, typewriter rentals, and maybe even a quiet place to go hide.

* **Special Collections**—Most any library will have some rooms set aside to one particular specialty. The *Hayden* library at Arizona State University has a solar energy special collection and an Arizona historical room, both of which stock fantastic and otherwise unavailable source materials. The trick is to find the library that has the collection you need. Usually there is a master state list of total library resources hidden in the office. This is the first place to check.

* **Serendipity**—Always make it a point to nose into *everything* in the library. Check the books that are going back on the shelves. See what's left on copy machines, look over shoulders, sample books totally at random, wander through unlocked doors, eavesdrop, and so on. So many times, I've found a whole new approach to a problem or a whole new world of information literally by tripping over it. Chance favors the prepared mind.

keeping informed—trade magazines

It never ceases to amaze me how many people never heard of trade magazines. Just about any field has *controlled circulation* magazines intended for a select group of insiders. While they are often free or at least reasonably priced to "qualified" subscribers, you'll never find them on a newsstand, they are rarely advertised, and they charge ludicrous prices to "non-qualified" readers.

Typical electronic examples include *Electronics, Electronic Design, EDN, Electronic News, Digital Design, Circuits Manufacturing, EE Times, Electronic Buyers News, Telecommunications, Electronic Components News, Electronic Products,* and a great heaping bunch more. Of this list, *Electronics* and *Electronic News* charge a subscription price; the rest are free.

Inside a trade magazine, you'll find lots of ads for the field. You can get more information on these ads by using the reader service bingo card. You'll also find lots of technical articles, but these may be lacking in quality or keyed to certain advertisers. You'll find trade journals useful to get product information and to find out what is current and what is mainstream in a particular field.

You qualify for these by requesting a form using your business letterhead to get a qualification card, and then telling them what they want to hear. No one to date has been tarred and feathered for willfully and maliciously filling out "that which is not so" on a qualification card. The controlled circulation requirements are to meet postal regulations for special rates. If you are interested in the ads, that's all that counts to the advertisers.

Many of these offer yearly directories and special issues that are extremely helpful in pinning down products and ideas. Any particular directory pretty much favors the advertisers in that magazine, so several are needed for a total picture.

Once you get on a list, or once you borrow someone else's copy of some useful trade magazine, use the reader service card. Keep the requests under twenty or so items per card. Use a "chief engineer" looking rubber stamp with your name and box number on it. Avoid street addresses since you are after information, not salesmen. Oh, yes, they will also want your title. Put down something like

> SR. PROD. DEV. ENG.

with a rubber stamp. Make sure your title is open to literal interpretation for a wide number of different money machines. Yes, I am definitely the head prod of my own money machine. So are you.

Make sure you expose yourself to every trade magazine that's useful to your money machine. Do this by personal subscription, by borrowing copies, or by using a library. Donate your older copies in turn to a library, school, or technical club. On anything you paid for, you can usually take a tax writeoff when you make the donation.

Besides trade journals, *any* magazine should have things of use to you in it. In addition to newsstand magazines, there are special interest magazines. Hobby computing alone now has fifteen major magazines. You'll find these via direct mail, in libraries, or by going to stores where the interest is featured, such as a retail computer store for computer magainzes, a food co-op for alternate lifestyle magazines, and so on.

No matter where you are, if there is a magazine nearby, pick it up and read it to see if it can help you. Such obvious places as medical offices, barbershops, waiting rooms, and so on should be an interesting source of supply. Make it a point each month to discover at least two new magazines which you never heard of before.

You'll also find scholarly heavyweight scientific journals. Examples include the *Proceedings of the IEEE, Solar Energy,* and thousands more. These usually cost a bunch and are often so erudite they don't contain anything directly useful to your money machine. Unless you want the prestige of belonging to these groups, always use a library or other "free" copy to avoid the $35 per year upward cost of these information sources.

My own favorite magazines? My top three of the one hundred and thirty-seven are *MAD, Co-Evolution Quarterly,* and *The Mother Earth News.* Glad you asked.

keeping informed—the feds

The federal government can be a good source of information. You probably know by now that you can send fifteen cents to them to find out why rutabagas are good for you. It turns out that 99 percent of what they have available is ordinary drivel, abject drivel, or can't even qualify as drivel. But there is so much printed that the remaining one percent will be a very large and most useful source.

Your starting place for just about everything is called the *Monthly Index of Government Publications* and costs around $6 per year if you don't use your library copy. It, and most everything else, is available from

> Superintendent of Documents
> U.S. Government Printing Office
> Washington, DC 20402

Here's a few other federal information sources I've personally found useful for my money machine:

Maps and aerial photographs:

> Denver Distribution Section USGS
> Denver Federal Center Bldg 25
> Denver, CO 80225

Government surplus sales:

> DOD Surplus Sales
> PO Box 1870
> Battle Creek, MI 40916

Backpacking and hiking information:

> National Park Service
> Interior Building
> Washington, DC 20240

> US Forest Service
> 1318 North Chambliss Street
> Alexandria, VA 22312

> US Bureau of Land Management
> C Street
> Washington, DC 20240

Radio and TV regulations:

> Federal Communications Commission
> 1919 M Street
> Washington, DC 20554

Patents:

> US Patent Office
> Crystal Palace
> Arlington, VA 20231

Tax information:

> Internal Revenue Service
> 1111 Constitution Avenue
> Washington, DC 20224

Standards:

> National Bureau of Standards
> Gaithersburg, MD 20760

Space technology:

> National Aeronautics and Space Administration
> 400 Maryland Avenue SW
> Washington, DC 20546

Geological information:

US Geological Survey
12201 Sunrise Valley Drive
Reston, VA 22092

Since there's a zillion different agencies, your own list of what's important will probably be different. Many of the Washington-area addresses will only refer you to something more local, so you can short circuit this run-around by checking the US Government listings of nearby big cities.

The cost of most bulletins and information is very low. Typical prices are in the dollar range. For instance, a copy of any patent costs you fifty cents. Just order by number.

Be sure to check your state as well to see what they have to offer. I've found the Agricultural Extension Service, the Bureau of Mines, the State Parks Board, and the state Natural Resources Council to be useful for my own money machine. You'll also want to check locally for things like zoning and building codes, city business license regulations, and so on.

keeping informed—be a book junky

Your money machine will work best if you are a book junky. You should have at least a five-dollar-a-day habit. Ten will be much more like it. Some of your main dealers will be bookstores. Recognize that you'll need several of them. These should include

* A technical one

* A name brand one

* A special interest one

* An escape reading source

* A used and exchange one

You'll also find important books in non-book stores that specialize in what your money machine is up to. Hobby computer stores stock all sorts of hardware and software books. Electronic distributors have lots of technical paperbacks available. Wool shops will have a selection of loom and weaving books. Tool outlets will have books on using lathes and specific construction projects. Lumber yards will have how-to pamphlets and plans. Remember that a bookstore is a place where you can buy books, not a building that has a sign that says "bookstore" out front.

You can find out about new titles by checking into *Forthcoming Books* at a library or bookstore. Or, you can carefully read reviews in magazines likely to cater to your needs. Or, you can and should collect your own set of publishers catalogs. You should also watch the "what's new" area of the stores you visit.

Should you want a book that's not immediately available, order it direct from the publisher or from a large, specialty mail order book service. Your direct order to the publisher gets processed just as fast as a local store's order does and fewer people are involved in the transaction. Another reason to deal direct is that most technical books are guaranteed. If you don't like what you get or it isn't what you want—send it back. It's easier dealing with a faceless publisher than a local store owner.

You can minimize your book costs by staying with paperbacks and used texts when you can, and exchanging with friends or others with the same interests. Books used in your money machine can often be tax deducted as a business expense. Out-of-date books can be exchanged for others at a used store or donated to a school or library.

Avoid the use of book clubs and books sold in entire sets. You are your own best judge of what you should be reading. No way should you let somebody else pre-package or pre-chew something for you.

keeping informed—getting product information

If your money machine is in any way involved with hardware, somehow you have to locate the bits and pieces you are going to use in your products. For instance, here are some of the things I've recently needed for my own money machine:

* A sack of fenugreek seeds

* A 3/32" end mill

* A fettling knife

* Sheets of .062 MD filled nylon

* A three stop neutral density filter

* A 200 psi, 200 in^3/min pneumatic source

* A 74LS640 octal bus transceiver

* A 7-1/2' topo of Dunton, Colorado

* A 15 dent beater bar reed

You can run a quick check on how good your product search abilities are by finding everything on this list. Nailing down the things you need is one of the black arts, if you are to be able to find things promptly, with little effort, and at reasonable prices. Things get even hairier if you only suspect that what you are after *may* exist.

A good starting place is the trade magazines. Heavily fill out the bingo cards and organize and save what comes back. Pay special attention to outfits who give you prices in their ads. Sources that you have to return to to find out how much something costs, or ones that send you a salesman instead, are *by definition* priced out of your market.

The trade magazines will often issue a yearly directory or buyers guide. Electronic examples are the *EEM Master,* the *Gold Book,* and the *Electronics Buyers Guide.* These have who-makes-what sections and where-who-is sections, along with the usual ads. For heavy reading* there's always the old standby *Thomas Registery of Manufacturers* in most libraries.

Try to find the major distributor or direct mail warehousing outfits and collect their catalogs as well. Some examples include *McMaster-Carr* for tools and industrial supplies; *WW Grainger* for motors and controls; *Small Parts* for mechanical stock; *Newark, Allied, Burstein-Applebee,* or *Cramer* for old-line distributor-type electronic parts; *Advance* for silk screen stuff; *Alvin* for drafting and drawing materials; *Forestry Supplies* for Woodsy Owl costumes; *Cadilliac* for industrial plastics; *Fischer Scientific* for expensive chemicals; and *Jensen Tool* for electronic tools. You'll probably have your own favorites, so build up as complete a catalog file as you can.

Be sure to check the popular "access" catalogs. The first and best are the *Whole Earth Catalog,* the *Whole Earth Epilog,* and the continuing updates in *Co-Evolution Quarterly.* There are a host of rip-off imitators of varying quality. Two more recent and useful access guides are *The Catalog of Kits and Plans* and *The Mail Order Craft Catalog.*

Look carefully for surplus and cut rate outfits. In computer electronics, there are usually two types. The first sells quality name brand components with full guarantees at prices well under those of franchised "old line" distributors. The second type offers "as is" seconds and distress stock at far lower prices. With the second type, you buys your ticket and you takes your chance. Parts from these super-cheap sources are useful to learn on and to build things for yourself, but they should never be designed into something that goes out the door, since the source may dry up or go sour. Both types of stores usually have full page ads in the backs of the hobby electronics magazines. For mechanical surplus check out the ads that appear in *Popular Science, Mechanix Illustrated,* and *Popular Mechanics.*

---

*Several hundred pounds worth

Check your local sources and get familiar with what they have. Use the *Yellow Pages,* and the alternate *People's Yellow Pages.* Watch your local freebie *White Sheet, Pennysaver, Green Sheets,* or whatever. Don't forget Sears. Above all find yourself a decent hardware store and a large hobby shop. Visit all the local junkyards and dumps, and pin down exactly what they have to offer.

But, if what you need isn't immediately available at the price you want, order direct to the manufacturer, and do it yourself. It *always* turns out cheaper to do things yourself, working direct, than it is to have somebody locally order something for you. It's always much quicker. On real heavy items, make sure your savings by ordering across the country aren't offset by stiff shipping charges. It may still be faster, but you might not save as much as you thought you were going to.

If you are given the choice between getting a dose of Bubonic Plague or talking to a salesman or manufacturer's rep, take the plague. You'll be way ahead. It pains me no end to have to try to look credible to some insecure salesman or rep while you try to get a few dollar parts to try out a new design. They will either ignore you if there isn't enough in it for them, or hound you if there is.

You should also avoid ever receiving any obviously expensive free samples. Either much will be expected of you in return, strings will be attached, or the samples are being given to you in hopes that you will use them instead of their competitor's better and much cheaper approach to the same problem. Sample requests are in order when what you need is some low cost item normally shipped only in large quantities and costing far less than the usual minimum factory billing.

Get in the habit of continuously requesting catalogs and product information. Send five letters or more a week. Use your business letterhead, and always make specific requests. Ask for pricing in reasonably high quantities to get their interest. Always write to the main plant, not to a local rep.

Some of the replies you get will be outrageous and should be framed for their humor value. Recently, I got a solenoid quote in which they wanted $250 for a usually free sample, and $10 for the beast in 25,000 lots. You can get better solenoids than theirs for a dollar in singles on the surplus market. Other replies will be reasonable and useful. Save these and use them for your product sources.

If you are having an unreasonably difficult time nailing some product down, maybe you should scrap this route and pick another. Some things seem to always be expensive, and for no apparent reasons. Anything optical, microwave, hydraulic or involving flow meters, lasers, pressure transducers or humidity sensors is almost guaranteed to be priced insanely high. If you can't find what you need in bargain catalogs like *Edmund Scientific* or *Airborne Sales,* chances are you will find the entry fee into these areas too stiff.

Always ask yourself if there isn't a better, cheaper, or easier way when digging out your own product sources.

keeping informed—stay in school forever

School should not be something that is turned on for the first few years of your life and then switched off and forgotten. Your whole life should be an educational and schooling process. The more you learn and the better you learn it, the better will be your string of money machines. As with anything else, the trick is to ferret out what is useful from the ripoffs.

You can easily argue for or against a formal college education. The benefits include a sheet of paper that gives you credibility, the fact that you learn to think for yourself, gain the ability to independently complete things on your own, and find a route to recognizing how and why you are being ripped off. The value of these last three items cannot be overemphasized. They are super-important for any money machine, and *extremely* hard to pick up elsewhere. Unfortunately, these often won't develop until well into a Master's level program.

The liabilities include a very high cost, the bad vibes of some inane courses taught by bumbling incompetents, and the loss of six or more years while others are plunging full speed ahead with their money machines.

Correspondence courses can also be a very bad ripoff. True, for some people in very unusual situations, they will prove of value. But these people would be much further ahead if they changed the special situation instead. The thinly disguised main purpose of electronic correspondence schools is to get the government to buy free color TV sets for veterans, nothing more. Due to limited cash flow, the quality of instruction is low, and a student failing is almost unheard of. Many of the schools are of, by, and for losers.

If you have been exposed to "formal" education, fine. Make the most of it. If not, *immediately* set up your own self-study program, arranging your curriculum to agree with what your money machine will need. And continue it forever.

Very useful types of courses are the special interest ones taught on the junior college level by doing dogger *part time* instructors. Of some 250 plus credit hours so far, including master's level work in two fields, my four most valuable courses have been

* Typing

* Technical Illustration

* Magazine Article Writing

* Basic Photography

It turns out one of these was a high school course, one junior college, one university level, and one a private and informal school. But similar things are regularly offered at most junior college and continuing education schools.

The first of these courses was free, while the others averaged $30 each. They have paid for themselves thousands and thousands of times over. On the other hand, I've yet to use Rademacher transforms in solving fifth order partial differential equations, or found a really good use for an ecological interpretation of Adena settlement patterns, despite their very high dollar and energy cost to me.

Something that's sure to surprise you is that the first few minutes of any new course will be as valuable to you as the whole rest of it put together. It's during this "first encounter" time that you learn new insights and trade secrets, professional inside ways of doing things, and a whole new ball game in general. So, watch for these crucial moments and extract everything you can from them.

Another key to education is that hands-on work is far more important to you than theory. Use, practice, and apply what you learn continually. No matter how many computer programming books you've read, you have accomplished nothing till you hang up the machine in a permanant loop, or output continuous "form feed" commands till the room is overflowing with confetti, or dump the entire main memory, or stand on the tape while the Teletype is loading it. You are no fireman till you have your first structural reburn because of a poor overhaul job, or have lost a quarter mile of hand-built line by not going down to mineral soil.

One sure way to learn is to jump into some money machine, only to find out later that you completely missed the basics. There's some physical law, a legal restriction, or a political hangup that makes what you are out to do essentially impossible. This is called doing things the hard way.

A far saner, cheaper, and better vibed route is to use schooling to inform yourself of these factors ahead of time. Find out what it is that will limit you doing what you want to with your money machine, and then either avoid the limits or recognize that you have a problem that can't be solved. At least not without a bunch of bad vibes and a loss of psychic energy. Let's look at some gotchas:

* So many alternate energy people either never heard of the laws of thermodynamics or else they expect Congress to repeal them.

* A computer or game product that glomps onto a TV set's antenna may be simple and cheap, but there are some totally inane, extremely expensive, and extremely time consuming FCC regulations that can prevent you from *ever* doing so.

* The Don't-Rock-The-Boat (DRTB) and the Not-Invented-Here (NIH) syndromes practically guarantee that you will never sell big business on any product improvement or new way of doing things.

* Change is often the last thing that many people or institutions ever want to see. This is true even if the change is "obviously" very much for the better.

* Paperwork and procedures can eat you alive in certain activities. This is particularly true of selling to the feds or working with the "educational" market in any way.

* Externalities may nail you to the wall. Just because your new laser stopwatch works beautifully on the bench, don't expect it to pick speedboats off a river or see through the dust on a rodeo ground.

* Existing sales and distribution channels may not open to you and may completely dominate the market.

Your schooling should include simple models and experiments of anything you want to get heavily into. The purpose of research is to use the minimum time, energy, dollars, and effort to get the effect you are after to show up at least reasonably well. Omit this model step and you will be sorry.

Teaching another is a very good learning process. Your students will force you to organize your material and then to master it. They will identify what is important, interesting, and understandable.

Don't overlook informal education. You get this in rap sessions, particularly those including as many doing doggers as possible. Surround yourself with winners and let some of their aura sluff off onto you. Join clubs where you can help others and others can help you. Become a member of organizations whose newsletters can help and whose training materials will be useful. Sop up all useful vibes, all scraps of information. Go to high energy scenes like trade fairs, exhibits, conferences.

Whatever else you do, stay in school forever. Only, be sure to very carefully define what school is and how it is going to reward you. Make it pay on a cash-and-carry basis. This is your biggest secret to keeping informed.

"You're a hippopotamus."

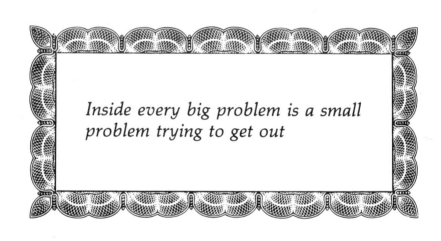

Inside every big problem is a small problem trying to get out

FIVE

Communications I—Words

Words-on-paper delivered out the door can be your crucial key to a winning money machine. Words-on-paper are almost always a very high personal value added product. They can be a near-perfect deferred income product, continuing on and on to generate royalties and future sales. The same words-on-paper, or at least similar ones, can be resold many times to many different people.

Words-on-paper are the key to the control of information flow between you and your customers. They form your image and will be all your customer has to go on if he never sees you. Even if your money machine doesn't directly offer words for sale as articles, plans, or books, you'll still need them to communicate with your suppliers and customers in the form of orders, receipts, catalogs, ad sheets, assembly manuals, parts lists, thank you notes, or whatever.

Now, I'm not about to sit here and tell you how to write. I do firmly believe that anyone can learn to write. This is even true of people with such severe handicaps as a background in journalism or English literature working against them. What I do want to do is show you what I think is important and what I think works in using words-on-paper to communicate. My important words-on-paper are mostly non-fiction articles, books, and how-to construction and assembly details, so that's what we will center this chapter on. But the same general ideas will easily carry over to just about anything you write.

Before we do look at what is important in words-on-paper, let's shatter a few myths. Another quiz:

Its very hard to break into print

True ☐   False ☐

The magazine article market is small

□ True   □ False

Its just about impossible to get a book published

□ True   □ False

Reject slips are a psychic energy sink

□ True   □ False

All false, of course. Remember the public serials list at your library from the last chapter? 20,000 periodicals. Assume they only appear once a month and all need only eleven articles per issue. That's 2,640,000 articles a year. Now, very conservatively assume the average pay is $125 per article and that each article goes 2000 words. That's over five *billion* words worth almost a third of a *billion* dollars. Year in and year out. And, that's only the magazines your library happens to stock. It doesn't include the zillions of others they don't stock, books, booklets, plans or paperbacks, much of fiction, or things published internally, for direct mail, or in other countries.

Most editors are desperate for *anything* of value to print. Each and every issue, forever and ever, they have this gaping maw to shovel articles into. Admittedly, a lot of these editors are swamped with lots of misinformed drivel and poorly conceived garbage that ignores totally what the editor wants or who his readers are. He may be up to his ears in this stuff. But that doesn't stop him from perpetually being short of good material.

For each and every overblown "general-interest"* newsstand magazine that fails, a dozen high energy special-use, special-interest magazines replace them. We've already seen how hobby computing alone has over fifteen major new magazines that didn't exist three years ago. Other examples of special-interest magazines are *Live Steam; Shuttle, Spindle, and Dyepot; Fire Engineering; Alternate Sources of Energy; California Geology;* and *WET-The Magazine of Gourmet Bathing.* There are, of course, thousands and thousands more.

Book publishers are in an even deeper bind. Seems they have this printing press. It can either eat manuscripts or gobble up interest dollars used to pay for the loans that bought the press. The press is forever starving for one or the other. Pressmen are high paid help and a good one is priceless. Unlike magazines, a current book list is continuously going out of date. Active new titles are essential for survival. So, it turns out that book publishers are also desperate for decent material. Most legitimate book publishers would like some assurance from you that you can write ahead of time, like a few articles in print,

---

*whatever that is

some sort of track record of previous work and so on. It's unthinkable to even *want* to write a book till you have done this background build-up anyway. The impossible-to-publish myth comes from people who either never looked at what a reader wants or think they can write a book before getting lesser things accepted and in print.

Ah yes, reject slips. Any time a publisher does not meet your current market needs, or has too poor a payment record, takes too long in responding, or whenever you are too busy on things more suited to your money machine, you may have to send a reject slip to a publisher. You shouldn't ever feel bad about having to send one to a publisher—it's just part of the everyday mechanics of writing.

My own reject slip I send out looks like this:

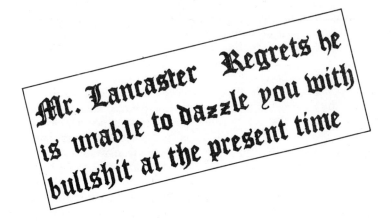

The market is there and it is desperate for your material. Let's go on and see what is important for your words-on-paper:

words—cannot stand alone; they must be integrated into a words plus pictures plus art plus layout package

Most people don't really like to read. A lot either can't or won't. Because of this, your message *must* be combined with attractive and clarifying figures, artwork, and photographs. Besides this, the layout of what you're presenting has to be attractively broken up. This is to first capture the reader's interest and later to hold him.

Words by themselves simply won't hack it. For your message to get across, you have to integrate words, pictures, captions, artwork, and layout into a complete package. We'll be expanding on this a bunch and looking at the non-word parts of your communications-on-paper package in the next chapter.

words —everything written must be your own effort

The object of the game is to maximize your personal value added to your words-on-paper. Your whole words + pictures + artwork package must be your own work if you are to add the maximum possible personal value to it. This means your own ideas, approach, outline, rough draft, format, final copy, corrections, rework, and final polish, along with your own corrections of page proofs and finals.

Stuff ripped off from another source always has aims and purposes different from yours. No way can it add to your particular message. It can only dilute what you are trying to deliver. Besides, anything easy to get is often pushing a second rate way of doing things as well.

What harm is there in letting somebody who is a "better" typist do your final copy? Just this. It is during the final copy that glaring errors become obvious; that omissions and wrong-way-around sequences hit you over the head; that bits of pieces of final polish can be added or removed. Doing your own final makes the difference between mediocre drivel and writing that has snap, reader interest, and reader retention. NEVER omit this crucial step of doing your own final copy. There is no one better than you to deliver your particular message.

Never collaborate with someone else while writing. You'll end up with a many headed monster and a total lack of continuity every time. It *is* a good idea to have others read and comment on your work. But, you should only pick up what you agree with and the people who do the reading shouldn't feel bad if you ignore them or do the exact opposite of what they suggest.

words—must fill a reader's hidden needs

Why do people read anyway? I think there are four main reasons:

* escape

* wish fulfillment

* ego reinforcement

* information

Some people may read for escape simply because they are bored or have nothing better to do. Others will actively seek out the-butler-did-it mysteries; Nazi-secret-U-Boat-attacks-Butte-Montana adventure; the-eggplant-that-ate-Chicago science fiction, bored-of-the-rings fantasy, or crawling-on-the-grass gothics* They may creatively use this escape reading as a break from their usual routine.

Much of humor and entertainment writing is also a form of escape writing.

People read for wish fulfillment by picking those magazines about what they would like to be rather than what they are. Those in scungy houses usually read the fancy house magazines. Aviation magazines are read by those not yet pilots. Maybe they can't even afford flying lessons. Financial magazines are read by people with little to invest. Travel and adventure magazines are often read by people who live on the 35th floor of an apartment building and have never been off the block, and so on.

A book or a magazine that is offering specific how-to information couldn't possibly survive on only those readers who actually *build* and *use* what is offered. These readers are a tiny minority. A very few others will modify the project for their own needs. Many will ignore the article and go on to the next one. But the vast majority of the readers will say, "Gee, that's great; someday I'd like to build one of those," or "Boy, I'd sure like to have the smarts and/or time and/or money to do that!" In other words, the story will provide a wish-fulfilling need.

Thus, while your story may purportedly be a detailed nuts-and-bolts how-to construction project, unless you provide for this wish-fulfillment need of the majority of your audience, you will lose them.

Reading for ego reinforcement takes place when the reader feels he is part of the team. A bugs-and-bunny freak like I am reading *Environmental Action*, a corporate polluter reading *Fortune*, a member reading his lodge magazine. All these go to the sources that they "believe" in and use the sources to reinforce this belief. There is a steady need to reinforce what people feel is important to them. So, your writing must make the reader feel like he is on the team, that he belongs, that he has done the right thing by stopping to read what you have to offer.

It sure would be simple if people only read for information. But, unfortunately, very few people do. So few, that they won't be able to support you, the book, or the magazine. Thus, you should always strive to fill these hidden needs of escape, wish fulfillment, and ego reinforcement as part of what you present. Fail to do this, and you will lose a lot of your audience.

---

*Gothics always have a dumpy female on the cover crawling on the grass outside a Charles Adams Victorian house; another characteristic is that the people's names are taken off interstate highway exit signs, e.g. Ludlow Amboy.

Two words I strongly believe in are "user oriented." So many books and articles are wrongly written

* to show the author is an expert
* to sell a second rate product or approach
* to shove a point of view down someone's throat
* to be easy to "teach" out of

All of these reasons completely ignore the reader and his needs. The key to acceptable writing is to be user oriented. Provide the reader with things he either needs or thinks he needs.

words—should be at the lowest possible level

Use the shortest words you can. Use the simplest sentences you can. Keep it understandable. Write at a low enough level that ten percent of your audience feels they are being "written down" to. Eschew neologisms.* Do everything you can to keep your writing understandable and easy for the reader to grasp.

You should also recognize that there are several different types of readers, and try to provide something for each of them. Your *average* reader will go through around 80 percent of your material and get pretty much what you intended out of it, maybe a little less. The *browsing* reader will only look at the pictures, headings, and captions. You should design these to (1) tell a simpler and quicker story, and (2) to suck the browser into actually stopping and seeing what you have to say.

The *serious student* is rare, but you can be his friend forever. He wants much more than you can give him. You can help him along with hints and implications of where your stuff is leading, along with source lists, bibliographies, and other references of where to go for more.

Keep it simple.

words—should be transparent

Transparency is an elusive quality in writing. There is no really good way to define transparent writing. Writing is transparent when the reader does not notice he is reading. When he feels the author is directly talking to him personally, or that some magical source of infor-

---

*write plain while you are at it

mation, entertainment, or escape is being laid at his feet at precisely the level he wants and needs. You've hit transparency when the reader wants to continue reading so bad he will resent any interruption for any reason.

If you let your reader stumble over words that are too big or too strange, you lose transparency. If you sound cute, coy, or condescending, you'll also blow it.

You lose transparency if you aim at the wrong reader. One way to do this is to place a story in the wrong magazine. Any magazine has an image of who their readers are and what their readers want. This image will color and distort the channel through which you are trying to communicate. Journalists call this a *slant*. For transparency, make sure your image of what the reader is and wants *matches* that of the magazine. The same goes for any other communications channel or media.

Another way to lose transparency is to charge too much for your writing or require too much dedication of time or energy from the reader for what you are offering. Keep your channel costs down.

The layout and form of the words on the page will also change the transparency. Attractive breaks here and there make for much easier reading and much less fatigue. Only don't get the brilliant idea to put math equations, long quotes, foreign words, or some poetry in as a break.

Such a break will be enjoyed by the reader. But, of course, he will completely ignore what is in the break and go on to the text beyond. Nobody, but nobody, reads math equations as part of a text. Few people dig poetry enough to stop as well. If things like this are important to you, set them aside in, of all things, a sidebar. Or a "the math behind" section; or an appendix; or something like this. So, always give the reader visual breaks when and where they work in with headings, use layout tricks, and so on, but never put anything in the break that you actually want read. The same goes for bunches and bunches of irrevelant footnotes*.

Transparency is something you will have to pin down for yourself. Watch your next week's worth of reading and decide what is transparent and what is not. Then see how the writers are getting transparency, and how you can use the same ideas and techniques for your own words-on-paper.

words—must be personal

To involve a reader, you have to let him know he is part of what you are saying. The most powerful way to do this is with the word

---
*Who, me?

YOU.

When you don't use it, imply it. Or use *your*. For variety, you can use *I* and *We*, but avoid the first person I when it looks like your own ego trip or gets tedious.

Stay away from the impersonal, third person approach to anything you write. So much technical writing turns out bland, dull, and uninspired because it does not involve the reader. If you aren't going to involve the reader, why should he bother to get involved at all?

Good writing should be dynamic. The most common word in the English language is *Uh*. Number two is *Er*. Yet, they don't appear in print very often. Things in print always seem to be in neat, concise sentences. But, people don't always talk in sentences. So use fragments. Write like you talk. Combine mostly sentences with other bits and pieces that can get your point across better. Or more efficiently. As with many things, fragments are a spice, not a mainstream way of doing things. But use them where they clarify or add snap.

Short paragraphs, too.

If something is "wrong" by English teacher or dictionary terms, but you like it, use it anyway. Someone pointed out to me that the indexes in the last chapter are supposed to be indices. Phooey. Gag. Some idiot way back when issued an edict that "data" is always plural. Double gag. Data **is** entered into a register. Not data are or datum is. Use it like it sounds good. If a dictionary word won't hack it, make up your own. Like others did with humongous*. Or, as a ferinstance, use ferinstance.

May the force be with you.

Several books back I snuck one over on the proofreaders. Would you believe Qwerty? It's the key arrangement on most typewriters. We now have a word with no "u" after the "q." Help stamp out dictionaries. Keep the language dynamic.

words—have form

A good editor can usually bail you out and salvage poor writing. He has to have a reason to do so, has to have the writing solidly supported with good artwork, and has to believe the effort is worth it to his readers. But, the better your words-on-paper, the better off will be the starting material the editor has, and the much better the final product.

You can call the actual arrangement of your words-on-paper its *form*. Your overall form has to be based on an approach, a slant, an angle, a direction, or a point of view. We have already seen how the

---

*meaning "not small." Named for Hugh Mongus, a 420 pound roving linebacker for the Houston Oilers.

form has to be at the lowest possible level and how there have to be several paths through the story for readers of different interest.

Obviously, the form must flow in some reasonable direction. This is usually from problem to solution, from earlier to later, from simple to complex, from beginning to end. A confused reader is a gone reader, so watch the sequence of your words-on-paper very closely.

Most of the writers reference books cost money and do more harm than good. English books are only useful to shore up a wobbly desk, and even then they are dangerous because of the radiations they send forth. A decent dictionary may be handy, but you should only use it once a month or so at most. Things like *Bartlett's Familiar Quotations* and *Roget's Thesaurus* actually are dangerous and do more damage than they cure. A writer has a bad case of Roget's syndrome when he uses the wrong word in the wrong domicile.

There is one book that is very useful. It used to be called *20,000 Words*. By now, the number is probably higher. You'll find this book at most office supply stores. It's pocket sized and costs very little. It lists only the words and their hyphenation. Occasionally they will throw in an ultra-simple definition when two words sound the same and might be confused. Plan on wearing out at least one of these per year. It will be your most useful source and the only writing book you will need.

An important rule in writing is **any word that is not helping you is hurting you.** If it isn't adding, take it off. Leave it out. Most poor writing contains three times the number of words needed to get the message across. A second rule is to **use the specific rather than the general.** Use sharp, precise words of exact meaning whenever you can.

You probably will want to explain all your key points in two totally different ways to make sure they are not missed. At the same time, you shouldn't load down your central ideas with extra detail, nuance, implications, and so on. Keep the main concepts simple. Keep them direct. Keep them uncluttered. Keep anything distracting and irrelevant away from the mainstream.

It's a good idea to alternate heavy and light messages. If one paragraph has some sticky and hard-to-grasp technical details in it, ease way off on the next one. Repeat what you said much simpler or throw in something related and very easy to understand. Pull the reader back into the mainstream every now and then. Make him belong or feel good. Change the lengths of your sentences. Some short, some long. Use fragments occasionally.

One thing that's super-easy to do is to use the same word over and over again, sentence after sentence. Or, to keep the same structure, say starting each of seven consecutive sentences with an adverb ending in *ly*. Watch for these mind-in-a-rut traps. They become most obvious if you set the work aside for a while and then return to it. Avoid starting several paragraphs with the same word, particularly "I." Don't jar the reader. At least not unintentionally.

The three old standbys of **anecdote** (tell a story); **analogy** (show something like it); and **example** (show what it's good for) are certain ways to add reader interest and to clarify your points. Make heavy use of them.

The best way to study form is to see how others do it. Read everything that's already in print in the field you are writing about. See how form helps and hurts the transparency. Rip off the winners. Avoid everything else.

words—have a plan

From the first idea for your words-on-paper to beyond their final delivery to the reader, you should have and follow a master plan. Your master plan should be efficient. It should be profitable. It should work the way you want it to. It should deliver the sharpest, most user-oriented message in the quickest and best way you know how. Your particular master plan will depend on what your secret money machine is up to, and where your words-on-paper are to appear.

The starting place is almost always a defined need or at least an idea for one. People often ask me, "Where do you get your ideas?" The stock reply is "I buy them for fifty cents per hundred pound bale in ten bale lots." Once you tune yourself into gathering information, ideas and identified needs will beat you over the head. They will overwhelm you. They are everywhere. The problem isn't finding ideas at all. The problem is filtering the far-too-many ideas on hand to find useful and profitable ones.

One important rule for starting money machines is to keep the ideas and needs you develop simple. Don't bother with your *opus maximus** Eighty percent of everything written is doggerel or drivel. Aim for the eighty-first percentile, and you'll be home free.

Zero in on ideas that solve a reader's problems, open a door for him, entertain him, or give him good vibes.

Once you have your need or idea, gather in as many hard facts and useful things about the idea you can. Test or personally verify everything possible. This is one reason so many electronic books are so bad. The authors simply pass on the circuits of others without bothering to see if they work, or trying to sort out what is useful, up to date, and innovative from what is ground out to promote some loser components. Know whereof you speak. Be accurate. Check and double-check. Get the facts down. Precisely.

---

*or your biggie, either

After your idea is pinned down, find a different way to present it to your reader. This is your gimmick, slant, approach, trip, point of view, whatever.

Then, jump in with both feet and start writing. Talk to the reader. Stay user oriented. Don't worry too much about your lead or the beginning or the introduction yet. Since you do not yet know what it it is you are going to say, save the final form of the introduction for later. For now, just throw together some sort of a beginning. Carefully tie in all the artwork and picture ideas to your writing.

When your rough copy is done, sit back and look at it. Take a break and look at it much later. Is this what you want? Is everything in order? Do you cover the ground you meant to? Will the reader care?

A good sign here is a hollow feeling, a heaving feeling of inadequacy. If you are proud of what you have at this point, you are in deep trouble. Flush it and start over.

Now, do your final artwork, following some of what the next chapter will tell us. *Over half your effort should go into artwork.* Complete all art, all captions. Make sure the art tells a story by itself, quicker and simpler than the text does. Stick the artwork up on a wall or a storyboard so you can see everything at once and in the right order.

From here, you can go to your final copy. Use an electric typewriter, preferably a correcting Selectric II, with a carbon or film ribbon. Use bond paper. Do the typing yourself. Be on the lookout for polish as you go along. Simplify, sharpen, eliminate, complete. Get rid of all loose ends. Have the story be complete in itself.

The next day, proof your work. Throw away any word that isn't essential. Take things off with *Liquid Paper* and put them back in with ink. Most editors are highly suspicious if they receive "perfect" copy; this tells him that the proofing is missing or poorly done. One exception is when camera-ready copy is needed; this is rare and you'll know about it ahead of time. All your artwork and captions will normally be redrawn to make them look better and to "infuse" the particular image the magazine or other channel is after.

If some key point is left off, throw in an extra page and change the numbering to match. If you don't find something missing, you've done something wrong. Have others look and comment. Use only what they offer of value.

When you get to the point that you feel you are whipping a dead horse, bundle everything up and send it out the door. One place only. Package it in a way that it will challenge the post office to find newer and better ways to destroy it. Keep a copy and record of every thing you send out.

Later on, sometimes much later on, you will get back page proofs or "galley copies" of what you wrote. If you don't get page proofs, stamp your feet and scream and holler till you do. *Demand proofs.* And proofs of everything, *including captions*. Make sure everything is the way you want it, but only change the things that are clearly wrong, and make even these changes in the simplest possible way. Changes at this point in time are *very* expensive, very hard, and take lots of time. But, if something is wrong, fix it before you make a half million copies of it.

The final part of your master plan is a follow-up. Try to find the response to your words. Read letters and other feedback. Observe results. Use what you have written as a base to expand on for bigger and better things. Find the weak points of your master plan and improve them. Continuously.

words—must sell

Your words-on-paper have to bring nickels back to you if they are to be of use to your money machine. To get the most nickels back, you want to spend as few of them as possible in the first place, want to aim for a high paying channel to put your words-on-paper, and want to find a way of putting it all together that has reasonable odds of your making it.

Non-fiction special-interest magazines are often a good starting point for words-on-paper nickels. Payment rates for a medium-size story with artwork will run from $75 to $1000, with values just under $200 being average for some markets.

Now, this is no way to hit the megabucks, unless you become both very efficient and very prolific. You can make things much more interesting by combining your words-on-paper into

* a special-interest story
* a book chapter
* a reprint service
* a source of how-to information
* as foot-in-the-door contacts
* as a tie-in for royalties
* as free advertising
* to offer a companion kit
* to promote a direct mail service

Done this way, the few hundred dollars per article gets much more attractive. Hobby electronics and personal computing magazines are a big and dynamic place to start into print, if you are into this sort of thing. Unfortunately, their payment rates are unconscionably low today, actually being less than a quarter what they were a decade ago, allowing for inflation. But it's a place to start.

At any rate, if you are new to getting in print, step one is to find out where your readers are. Study the magazines you subscribe to or know about first. Check into a book called *Writers Market*. It lists many thousands of places to send words-on-paper, tells you how much they pay, what you need in the way of artwork, who to contact, and so on. You can also use the public serials list and the periodicals dictionary at your library for ideas on suitable magazines to use.

Regardless of where you get the idea for a particular magazine, you *must* check out a few current issues in detail. Read the fine print under the masthead to find out who is doing what at the magazine. Read the even finer print down below to get clues on whether they buy stuff from others. Circulation information can be picked up in the post-office-required notice that always has to appear in a winter issue, usually December or January. The periodicals dictionary may also have this information.

The reason for all this is to identify the reader you are aiming at. Another ploy is to request both an authors guide and an advertising rate card from the magazine. You can only reach the reader through the magazine, so what you want to do and say has to fit in with what the magazine thinks its readers want. Reading the ads will often give you an accurate picture of who the' magazine thinks its readers are.

There are several ways to send in a story. Simplest and best is to just send it in, **one place at a time,** along with return postage. You have to assume the publisher is honest. To not do so is such a psychic energy sink that it is certain to lead to bad vibes. Don't sweat copyright. You are protected already. More on this later.

Keep your first attempts small and simple enough that they don't tie up weeks and weeks of work, fancy artwork, special research, or expensive photos.

It's possible to send a *query* to an editor to find out if he is interested in something. This is usually a waste of both your and the editor's time. The editor would rather see the story than talk to you about it. A good query letter should be as hard to write or harder than the story will be anyway. If you must send a query, keep its length under half a page and zero in on why the editor's readers have a problem and how you are solving it for them.

Never work through an agent. The only known purpose of literary agents is to line up mediocre writers with nondescript publishers. Agents will severely damage your credibility in any special-interest market. Stay completely away from them.

One good break-into-print idea is to use fillers and very short items of reader interest. Magazines have a continuing need for things to put in loose ends around the issue. If your items are very short, such as tips and techniques, send in eight or so at a time. Most of them will get accepted, a few returned. If you do put together a dozen things, don't even send in your worst four. Be your own most critical editor.

Decent magazines will tell you almost right away that they have gotten your material, and usually pay on acceptance. Acceptance usually means a month to six weeks. Some cheaper outfits pay on publication and should be avoided. Watch out for any magazine trying to use a "binder fee" on you and run away from them. A binder fee keeps something the magazine can't afford out of its competitor's hands. They call it "insurance." I call it something else.

The larger cold cash dollars eventually turn up in the book field. Last year, I got over twenty times the nickels from book people than from magazine editors. As we have seen, you shouldn't even think about anything book length till you are solidly in print with shorter stuff, well exposed, and well paid.

There are three main routes to getting a book published. The first is through a *legitimate* publisher. These are contacted with a query, a complete outline, a sample key chapter, and some clues as to who you are. They will return a contract to you if they like what they see. The contract guarantees they will publish the book if you deliver it to them by a certain date. Usually, they will provide for a royalty that's based on how well the books sell. Something like nine or ten percent of the retail price is typical, less for the first few copies. Writing at a fixed fee for a book publisher is usually a ripoff and should be avoided.

There are no charges involved with a legitimate publisher. They cover all the costs of layout, printing, distribution, sales, advertising, the whole bit. They might even offer you an advance against royalties. You should avoid these advances. If you fail to deliver, or if the book bombs, the advance has to go back. The advance is another one of those fixed obligations that your money machine should stay away from.

A *vanity* publisher is a different deal entirely. You send him the story and several thousand dollars. He sends you back a pile of books you can sell anyway you like. These are the people behind those too-good-to-be-true little "publisher desperately needs books" ads in the back of many magazines.

Vanity press titles tend to be ignored by distributors, bookstores, and reviewers. This is because so many vanity titles can't even qualify as drivel, having a total market of three copies—the author, his agent, and his mother. Use of a vanity offprint will hurt you when it comes time to promote or sell your finished books.

A third route is to *self*-publish. You put the whole trip together your-self, finding a way to get the editing, layout, typesetting, printing, bind-ing, sales, and distribution done on your own. In exchange for all this hassle, you get the author's royalty, the publisher's profit, the distribu-tor's profit, and the retailer's profit. Not bad.

That's assuming you ever break even, which is highly unlikely. Oth-erwise, you get the author's loss, the publisher's loss, the distributor's loss, and the retailer's loss. Very ungood. If you do self-publish, get one of the good books on it, try something simple first, and only assemble and bind a portion of what you print. Good luck.

Good old common sense is the key to selling your words-on-paper. First, know who the reader will be. Write directly to and for him. Then, find a channel that gets the message from you to your reader as trans-parently, reliably, and profitably as possible.

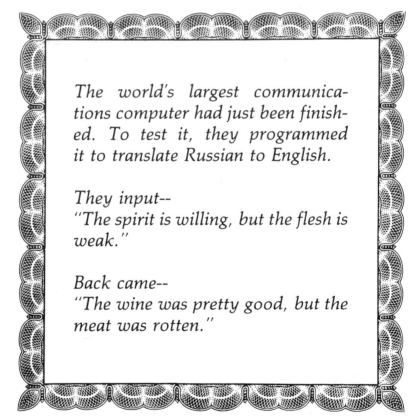

The world's largest communica-tions computer had just been finish-ed. To test it, they programmed it to translate Russian to English.

They input--
"The spirit is willing, but the flesh is weak."

Back came--
"The wine was pretty good, but the meat was rotten."

SIX

Communications II – Images

Images are the non-verbal parts of your on-paper communications. These can include photographs, graphics, artwork, illustration, layout, charts, typography, tables, and anything else that looks good and gets a message across. Your images can be as simple as some white space breaking up your message into bite-sized chunks or as complex as a commissioned portrait or other limited edition of art.

Since people more often like to look at pictures than read, your images are a very important part of your on-paper communications. Let's see what's involved in getting images working for you and your money machine:

images—cannot stand alone; they must be integrated into a words-plus-pictures total package

Sound familiar? That's what we said last chapter only insided out. Words won't hack it by themselves. Neither will straight pictures or any other single image form. You have to combine everything together into an overall package that works.

Half and half is often a good rule. This means half the final space goes for images and half for words. If you are heavy into a word trip, this means that much more than half your effort should go into the pictures. If you are a nature photographer or have some other high-image-content money machine, then most of your effort should go into words, captions, and continuity.

For most of my books, I personally aim for this 50-50 mixture. My usual drawings, printed-circuit layouts, schematics, and graphs won't lend themselves too well to this particular book. Instead, we've used the end-of-chapter cameos, the typography, the layout, the cartoons,

95

and the visual breaks to give the same effect.* Apparently it's working, because you've gotten this far.

On a typical special-interest magazine article, a combination of 2500 words or so and six visuals can be a good idea. This says a picture is worth 416.667 words rather than the usual thousand. Half the spread ends up on visuals, half on words this way.

Your visuals should be a mix of different images. Maybe an overall subject photo, a main drawing or schematic; a parts list, a detail shown as a tech illustration, a how-this-fits-into-the-big-picture block diagram, and some fancy typography and artwork used for your lead. You should use as much variety as possible, but make sure that everything "belongs" to the overall image trip you are putting together.

Your visuals rarely have to be ready for reproduction. If they have to be camera ready, you'll know about this ahead of time. All you usually need is something clear enough and understandable enough that one of the staff artists can go ahead and do final art for you without having to ask his boss dumb questions. In fact, if you do too good a job on your images, it may even hurt you. Here, the editor can ripoff your stuff and use it directly, rather than having an artist redo it. Unless you are fantastically good at images, this can lower the overall quality and appearance of what you are trying to do, particularly if your message has to fit in with several others in the same channel.

Obviously, if your main money machine trip is photography, cartooning, or other graphic illustrations, your images are your main product, and your approach will be different than this balanced mix that works for everybody else. Your main problem will probably be the words and the continuity rather than the images.

images—draw a line around some words

The simplest and cheapest visual you can do is to put a box around some words. Printers call this a *box rule.* When you do this, your words change into visual

* parts lists

* directories of suppliers

* charts of values

* ways to reemphasize your main points

* graphs

---

*Even those dumb footnotes are part of the visuals.

* end-of-chapter cameos
* how-to instructions
* catalogs of devices
* sequences of options

One of the sneakier uses for your words-in-a-box is to give your reader something he will want to save. Anything of apparent future value to him will do the trick. All it takes is a "Hey, I can use this!", or a "This looks like something I ought to hold on to," and you are home free.

The foremost rule of your box-around-some-words is to keep it clean. Use as few words as possible, chosen as succinctly as you can. Break long lists into easily viewed groups of four or five entries. Use lots of "daylight" around the words and numbers. Separate things into well defined columns, rows, or paragraph-like groupings. Use lines to separate if you have to, but try to do the job with plain old white space as much as you can.

---

the sidebar:

A *sidebar* is a very useful words-in-a-box trick you can use to present something out of the mainstream of your message.

Sidebars are handy to give your readers a short tutorial background. You can use them to show alternatives to what you are trying to say. They can indicate how your message fits into the big picture. If you have something else to say that doesn't seem to "fit" in the main message, a sidebar can often bail you out.

The words in a sidebar may be set in finer print than the main message. Figures and artwork can and should be included but use only one or two and keep them very simple and very direct.

If your words-in-a-box involve computer software or listings, some extra caution is called for. Since computers are dumber than people*, they are *very* fussy over every last little detail of punctuation, sequence, spacing, and so on. If at all possible, have the original working computer do your final art. This eliminates the errors that creep in between computer, programmer, author, editor, typesetter, and paste-up. Admittedly most computer printouts look awful. You can improve them quite a bit by using a better quality printer to start with. While your words-in-a-box should always be attractive and readable, your first goal should be accuracy in the case of computer printout.

Graphs combine several words-in-a-box with lots more lines. Your graphs should be very clean, using only as much resolution as you

---

*but smarter than programmers

barely need to get by. The thing that's not changing goes across the bottom, while the result goes up and down. Both should be clearly labeled. Not only "what" but "how much per unit" as well. Use a sensible number of divisions, often 1, 2, or 5 units. Use a *linear* graph where the absolute amount of things are important to you; use *semilog* graphs where the percentage changes are of main interest. A one dollar change in a stock will always be the same size on a linear graph, regardless of stock price. A ten percent change in stock price will always be the same size on a semilog graph, no matter how much the stock costs.

If you are going to use several graphs, make up a background once, and then copy it and add details as often as you need to. It's reasonable to chop off the bottom of a graph to emphasize only the variation, but this gets to be dirty pool if you chop so much off that something which is only changing a little looks like it is skyrocketing or nosediving. Always provide an example of some sort so the reader knows how to read your graph and then be able to use it himself.

images—secrets of line art

Line Art is anything you want to appear on the printed page that is solidly black or white. Examples include technical illustrations, cartoons, artist's line renderings, ad images, schematic diagrams, printed-circuit layouts, typography, headlines, maps, calligraphy, graphs, and so on. Despite the obvious differences of all these line art techniques, there's really only a few key secret rules to use:

* **Always use a much larger original than your final size.** Keep things big enough that you can see what you are doing and can conveniently work on small details. Then reduce the final size to fit the available space. As things are reduced, small irregularities go away and the quality always seems to go up. But, watch your line weights since they change apparent size as they get reduced. To beat this, always work to the same size and key your line weights to the best final result on your reduced copy. Artists and layout people often work one-third to one-half larger than the final. Printed-circuit artwork is usually done *twice* normal size for usual layouts and *four times* normal size where extreme accuracy or close tolerance is involved.

* **Always retrace your final artwork.** This is the only way you can completely eliminate all guidelines, mistakes, corrections, background problems, ghosts, and so on. Things go much easier and

much faster if you assume from the start that a final clean copy will be made.

* **Use crutches.** A crutch is anything that makes your life simpler, easier, or less of a hassle. Anything that helps goes. Never mind if it is dirty pool. Only the result counts. Here's a few typical crutches:

* blue gridded paper that drops out

* a single master form reused

* instant transfer lettering

* line art "clip books" and "cheat books"

* using tape instead of ink

* templates

* stock symbols such as PC patterns or shading

* an opaque projector

* ripping off someone else's work, then changing it

* a light box for tracing

* cut, paste, and snip scissors drafting

* automatic lettering machines

* phototypesetting

* using the same artwork over many times

* **Be Efficient.** Show only the essentials, using the minimum number of lines you have to in order to get the job done. If it isn't essential, leave it off, remove it, cut it out. Avoid any confusion between things in front of each other by breaking up anything in back and emphasizing what goes in the front.

A *technical illustration* is one form of line art. Let's look at an example to see how these secrets work.

Here's the way I sent a technical illustration into Sams:

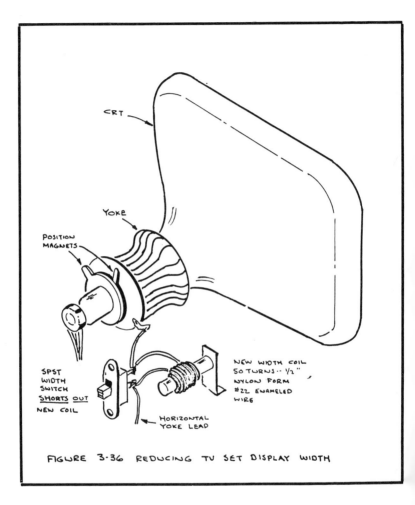

POSITION MAGNETS

YOKE

CRT

SPST WIDTH SWITCH SHORTS OUT NEW COIL

NEW WIDTH COIL 50 TURNS -- 1/2" NYLON FORM #22 ENAMELED WIRE

HORIZONTAL YOKE LEAD

FIGURE 3-36 REDUCING TV SET DISPLAY WIDTH

This particular tech illustration shows you how to reduce the width of a TV display so you can put characters from your computer on it. If you actually look into the back of a set, you'll find a royal mess. The illustration extracts only what is important. On the picture tube, only the essential number of lines are used. Uninvolved connections are only suggested.

And here is what they did to it:

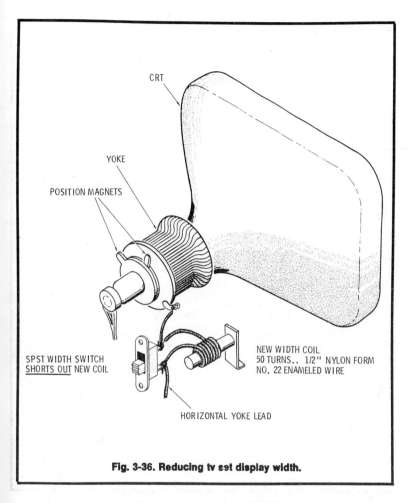

CRT

YOKE

POSITION MAGNETS

SPST WIDTH SWITCH
SHORTS OUT NEW COIL

NEW WIDTH COIL
50 TURNS.. 1/2" NYLON FORM
NO. 22 ENAMELED WIRE

HORIZONTAL YOKE LEAD

Fig. 3-36. Reducing tv set display width.

Details like the tube mount, the high voltage connector, other wires, internal gun structure, and so on are eliminated. These extras only confuse and should be left off. The position magnets may appear as extras, but they are used to clarify another point in the text that goes with this illustration. Note particularly how the lines behind other lines are broken to avoid visual confusion.

Here is a detail that shows us how the staff artist cleaned up the original: Once again, notice how the broken lines help the clarity.

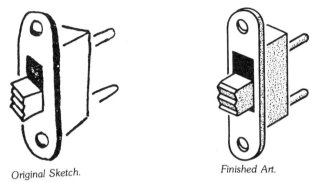

Original Sketch.   Finished Art.

The drawing started off with a TV set in front of it, and another tech illustration from a kit manufacturer was used as a crutch. Unfortunately, the other illustration was at the wrong angle and showed the wrong things, but it was useful to point out what the essentials were. The illustration was first drawn on an *isometric* grid, starting out with circles drawn with an isometric ellipse set. Isometric is OK for things like this, but will look distorted for boxy subjects. These should be done in true perspective, or else you can *foreshorten* just by cutting corners to get the same effect.

My final art was then traced onto a gridded 8-½ x 11 sheet. The grid makes the lettering straight and the borders square. I work directly in ink, using only a fineline and a regular felt tip pen. Incidentally, the only difference between these and a $50 technical fountain pen set is $49 and the fact that the technical pen set is forever clogging and making a mess. If you do work directly in ink, space your templates off the sheet slightly. The old dodge of taping dimes on the templates works, but is much thicker than you really need for felt tip pens. I use some nylon washer samples instead. Corrections are done with *liquid paper* or simply scraping the ink away with an *X-Acto* knife.

A Xerox copy is then made of the final that drops out the blue gridding, blobs of liquid paper, and so on. This is then sent to the publisher.

Pay attention to the other forms of line art you see around you and see how they apply these same rules to get good results that communicate effectively.

images—find a litho camera and use it

There are two entirely different types of photography. You may not even have heard of the second type, but it is far more important to your images and words-on-paper than the usual cameras of the *Instamatic* and *Polaroid* ilk. This other type of photography is called *litho photography*. A litho camera is usually immense. Many are so big that a darkroom is built into one end.

Litho cameras are used to very accurately change the sizes of artwork. Most often, they are used to reduce a larger original into a final size. Litho negatives or positives are all completely clear or completely black. There is no grey, no halfway. This type of negative or positive is essential for anything printed anywhere.

So, where do you find a litho camera? Well, you can start in the yellow pages under "lithographers." Or, just ask any printer, silk screener, anyone into electronic printed circuits, any newspaper, any magazine, any ad agency, any art department. Since these beasts usually go for two kilobucks or more, not counting the supplies and space, it's best to use somebody else's camera. Normal charges for a routine litho negative are a few dollars.

My main uses for litho photography are to reduce printed-circuit masters and overlays from the 2:1 size of the artwork. These become the negatives that directly give me the actual printed-circuit boards, and positives for silk screens that give me the component callout overlays. I also use the litho camera for dialplates, decals, instant transfer letters, meter faces, and labels, using the *Scotchcal, Metalphoto, Kepro,* and *INT* systems. Anytime you want to accurately change the size of something, or make it into something all black or all white, litho photography is the only way to go.

Unless you know the litho people very well, make sure they understand exactly what you want. Once I was charged $2.40 for the lettering front of a single sided PC board and $35 for the circuit foil patterns on the rear. Thinking this rather strange, I asked them about it. They explained that the front was an overlay that they ran to normal "set and shoot" accuracy, but that they "always" did their printed-circuit reductions to extreme accuracy since another customer into aerospace electronics demanded it.

Too little accuracy can be just as bad. It might not matter much on a T-shirt, but it can get downright messy for things that demand more precision. I had to run some PC boards that had to exactly match a 36-pin connector. If the reduction error was anywhere near half a part in 36, the pads would short out. It turns out that the litho guy simply turned his camera wheels to a big mark that said "50 percent" instead of measuring the actual reduction. This led to big trouble. I got around this by giving him a connector and telling him to hold it up to the ground glass and "make it fit." No more problems.

Always make sure you show the exact size you want your final shot reduced to before you order any litho work. Give them two well marked points to measure from. If things have to match up, give them a dimension on one piece of artwork and mark the others "shoot at identical settings." Better yet, try to get them all onto the camera at once and shoot them all at the same time; then cut the film up into individual pieces.

Another important use of litho cameras is for the *halftones* essential anytime you want a picture or something else with grey scale to appear on a printed page. There is only one way to print something and have it turn out truly grey on the page. And that is to use grey ink. And each different shade of grey will take a different color ink and a different pass through the press.

Since this is obviously ungood, we have to fake grey anytime we want it. Now, this may look grey:

but it really isn't. Magnify it, and you'll see something like this:

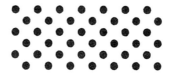

Any photograph or any continuous tone artwork has to be converted to these little dots before they can appear on a printed page. By pulling some tricks with a litho camera, you can make a *halftone* image that automatically converts a photograph into tiny dots as needed. You can do this with a screen that has a bunch of little holes in it, or there are several other ways. Which way you go, the cost, and the results depend on the quality you need, what type of press is in use, the ink and paper combination, and the number of copies you have to print.

Usually, a printer or publisher will do halftones for you, but this is a process you should know about, especially if you are going to self-publish or work with a small or inexperienced printing outfit. Poorly done halftones are certain to give you muddy results.

images—get your own photography under control

Good old slopping in the slush. I detest photography. Hate. Hate. Hate. No matter how hard I try, it always turns out unpleasant. In fact, the only time photography turns out worse than my doing it myself is when I have somebody else do it for me.

Then it turns out even more badder, costs a bundle, isn't at all what I wanted, and takes forever.

Being able to do your own photos for your on-paper communications is a tremendous, if painful, way to add personal value to your products. As with typing your final copies of all your words, doing your final prints on all your photos is a key to maximizing your value added.

Almost certainly, you should only use black and white photography. This is what is used in the overwhelming majority of everything printed, for the simple reason that it is cheaper and takes only a single pass through the press. A lot of what look like color in magazines is simply second-pass blocks of solid color or tints. So, color is out—unless you are a nature photographer trying to hit *Arizona Highways,* are into portraiture, or some other high quality money machine that demands color as part of its main trip.

You should use a big camera. Instamatics won't hack it. I don't like 35 millimeter. It isn't flexible enough, swings and tilts are nonexistent, and if you crop in the darkroom, you have to enlarge a bunch. Admittedly, if you are running Niagara Falls in a kayak, hang-gliding Whitney, or dropping El Sotano, a smaller camera might be an advantage.

We use a very old 2¼ *Rolleiflex* twin-lens reflex camera for scientific field work and outdoor travel shots. Our main studio camera is a 4 × 5 *Calumet* view, modified for small object photography by a long bellows and a process lens. The most common photo needed here is a detail of an electronic project or component. These are usually done on a translucent light box. The light box gives you shadowless photography since the subject is illuminated from the front with flash or floods and from behind with fluorescents. The swings and tilts on the view camera give you good control of distortion, composition, and depth of field. Hotspots are normally controlled with dulling spray applied very sparingly. Sometimes very white or black things are prepainted yellow or dark blue to reduce the subject contrast.

There are two recent developments in black and white photography that have made life far easier and simpler.

One of these is *Polaroid* type 665 film. Now, their ads notwithstanding, no way is a Polaroid print useful for reproduction. It is far too crude in resolution and has a miserable grey scale, besides disallowing all the tricks you can pull with an enlarger to make a better print. But the 665 gives you a negative as well. The negative is very easy to scratch and has only a modest resolution and grey scale, but it is super easy to use and adequate for most routine images-on-paper needs.

The nice thing about the 665 negative is that it gives you something usable with a minimum of slush-slopping and no darkroom. You also get a print immediately that tells you whether you have made any major boo-boos. The negative is processed by putting it into a bucket of glop (sodium sulfite) for a minute and then washing it. In daylight. A hardening step will help the scratch resistance, but you still have to be extra careful. The best negative exposure is with a slightly washed-out print.

So that's half the mess minimized. No more old-style darkroom tanks, or develop-short-stop-fix-wash hassles. All are magically gone.

Some stuff called *resin coated paper* minimizes the second half of the mess. *Kodabrome* is typical. You print this paper for 10 seconds and then tray-develop it for one minute, fix it for two, and wash it for five. You then hang it up to drip dry. No longer do you need a print dryer or the hassle of washing things forever. Print curling is gone completely. There are five grades of paper, all with the same speed except for two which are one stop slower than the others. Grades include soft, normal, hard, extra hard, and ultra. Ultra is litho paper. I use a lot of it to reproduce printed circuit 1:1 patterns and artwork overlays.

About the only expensive beast required is an enlarger. Besides this, a few trays, a timer, a printing easel, and a darkroom, and some way to wash is all you really need. My print washer is a Kodak automatic siphon (around $10) that sits in the bottom of a stall shower. My darkroom isn't quite light-tight so I only print at night. I've added a paper safe and a contact printer for convenience, some screens for special effects, and that's about all.

There are a few key secrets to slush-slopping. One is to keep the dry and wet sides of the darkroom forever separate. A second is to pay extreme attention to detail. Keep things clean. Spend extra time focusing. Watch your times and temperatures closely. Use distilled water if the city water is full of salt or rocks. Don't try to stretch chemicals; use fresh often.

Once you're into this mess, you'll undoubtedly be unhappy with your results. One thing that can help a bunch is to selectively enhance prints as you print them. Holding back light where you want things lighter is called *dodging;* you do this with your hands or a homemade dodging paddle. Adding extra light where you want things darker is called *burning:* a piece of cardboard with a hole in it is one way to do this. When dodging or burning, you have to keep moving to prevent any obvious ghosts or edges. Cut masks can also help. A red filter on your enlarger lets you see the image without exposing the print paper.

One way to get good pictures is to use the shotgun method. Take several hundred photos. One or two of them is bound to turn out right. When photographing people, don't even bother putting film in the camera till you have taken several dozen shots and they are ignoring you. Watch your composition. Keep something in the foreground; never split anything down the middle; don't let telephone poles grow out of people's ears; and so on. Hold steady. Get the lighting and the exposure right. Crop close to your subject during exposure. Crop even closer when you make your final print. Any part of the picture not adding is removing. Contrast tends to increase with printing processes, so submit prints that are slightly thin, unless you want lots and lots of contrast. Use a yellow filter for normal outdoor shots with sky; for extremely dramatic sky effects, use a red filter or a polarizing filter "tuned" to get the clouds to jump out at you.

Keep concise records of all your photo work. That way, you'll always be making new mistakes instead of repeating the same old ones over and over again.

images—make typography work for you

It's not just what you say that counts—it's how you say it as well. The shape and size of the letters you use, how they are combined together, and the image they convey says as much if not more than your message itself.

Tune yourself into typography. Read the *Art Directors Work Book of Type Faces*. Collect all the instant transfer lettering catalogs. But note that the latter often will slightly modify a standard font and put their own name on it so you think you have to get it from a single source. Collect some fonts that turn you on. Pay attention to other people's use of letters and see what is working and what isn't.

The particular font you use sets the overall style. For instance, see how the style and image go together in these examples:

Scholary	Informal
Western	Nineteen Twenties
Religious	COMPUTER
DIGNIFIED	Personal
Nervous	**Sturdy**

Things get downright absurd if you pick exactly the wrong font:

MACRO-The Man's Magazine
of BLOOD, GUTS, and GORE

Bad, isn't it? You can also pick fonts for different amounts of legibility:

Very Legible Type Font

nOT SO LEGIBLE TYPE FOnT

You use less-than-perfect legibility when you want the reader to slow down and absorb the vibes of the font. Available fonts group themselves into *Serif* fonts having those funny little feet on the top and bottom, *San-Serif* fonts with usually square tops and bottoms, and *decorative* fonts that cover just about anything left. The classic serif font is called *Roman;* the classic sans-serif one is called *Gothic.* The reason for the serifs goes back to when the words were carved in stone. It was too hard to get the tops and bottoms of every letter to come out the same height unless a serif was added.

You can change the size of the font to match the space you have available. Font sizes are measured in *points.*

six point

ten point

eighteen point

twenty-four point

thirty-six point

For a given type size and font, we have various degrees of *boldness,* the ratio of how wide the lines are compared to the spaces between the lines:

Light	**Bold**
Medium	**Extra Bold**

We also have a squashedness factor:

Condensed   Medium   Expanded

And, if we like, we can lean on our font a bit:

Normal Font   Italic Font

or mix cases:

UPPER CASE ONLY

Combined Upper and Lower Case

lower case only

You can greatly improve your message by watching your spacing:

Visually attractive spacing

Equal or Mechanical spacing

Poorly done   spacing

Your best source for typography is the instant transfer letters you can get at artist supply stores. There are many different brands. You can also get expensive automatic lettering machines if you get into large quantities of typography. But these machines cost a bunch, and you are out as much as $50 each time you change font or size. I use an old beast called a *Varityper Headliner,* mostly for my printed-circuit board callouts and overlays. A disc the size of a phono record goes on the machine to set the size and font; a strip of 35 millimeter photographic paper is output automatically following some wet-process slush-slopping. There are newer and more expensive ways to do the same thing. If you are near a large city, you should be able to find a firm that specializes in phototypesetting services. Printers will often be able to do the same thing, but at higher cost and with a more limited choice of fonts and sizes.

images—watch your advertising

Somehow, you have to let others know you exist. The best advertising you can possibly get is from satisfied customers by word of mouth. The second best advertising is anything that is free. You can get free advertising by

* Sending new product releases to trade magazines

* Writing a tech article that explains your product

* Making your products obviously yours with a distinctive style or logo

* Getting others to advertise your product for you as part of their money machine

* Having the promoters of an exposition or conference plug you as part of their promotion

* Demonstrating at fairs and clubs

* Letting your products advertise each other

So many starting money machines go completely overboard on expensive and misconceived advertising. Traditional ads are something to only approach very gingerly and then only when they obviously pay for themselves. Start out small. Use classified or very tiny display ads, till you are sure that you can benefit at all from ads.

If you have a really good money machine, you shouldn't need any ads at all. In my own money machine, I have to UN-advertise. I have an unlisted phone and an unlisted address located on a sand dune you can't get to. I rarely answer mail and am often away from any phone for months on end. In fact, there's lots of times when a steep twelve mile backpack or two carbide changes worth of caving is the only way to reach me. This lets me do what I feel is important for the clients I want to work with.

But, that's my trip. Your trip may call for some display advertising. But, use very little of it and test it first before you commit yourself heavily. Small ads that repeat often usually pull better than a one-shot heavy promotion. Watch your cost per thousand—and make sure the thousand are really people who need your product and can pay for it.

Your ads should have a clear and simple message. They need a *hook* that grabs the reader and attracts his attention. Your ads should have an easy way for the reader to respond, such as a mail-it-in coupon, a reader service number, a telephone that accepts charge cards, or something similiar.

Ad people have a stock "AIDA" formula for success. First get their ATTENTION. Then tell them more to get their INTEREST up. Then create a DESIRE to act by telling them what is in it for them. Finally use a response coupon or whatever to get their ACTION.

Have your ads deal with specifics of what you have available, what its features are, and, above all, how much your products cost. Try to give something "free" or nearly free away. Things like an instruction booklet, a directory, a handy use guide, a sample, or something else you just barely break even on that the reader will think is a super enough bargain to stop and respond to immediately.

Under NO circumstances should you use your ads to grab a larger part of a parity market from your competitors. You should not use ads to build an "image," whatever that is. Concentrate on specifics. I have this and will sell it to you for so much.

Last, but by no means least, never advertise something that you hope will be ready by the time the ad appears in print. First, it won't be ready. This is for sure. Secondly, you will hack off your customers, the exact opposite of what your ad is suppose to do. If you aren't ready, don't tell anyone you are.

Deeper Meanings #36

From Whack Your Porcupine Copyright ©
B. Kliban 1977. Workman Publishing,
New York, NY. Reprinted by arrangement
with the publisher.

Some Unmatters

Now that we've seen some of the key secrets to getting your money machine's information flow under control, let's go back to the mainstream to see what is and is not important in the way of legal matters, taxes, and "investments."

There are two types of *unmatters* we should look at next. Unmatters of the first kind are those things that other people think should be important for your money machine but really are not. Unmatters of the second kind are things so obvious and based on everyday common sense that we shouldn't really even have to mention them. But, we're gonna anyway.

unmatter—get it in writing

Anytime you do anything that is going to involve a bunch of your nickels, time, or energy, get it in writing. Verbal promises or understood agreements simply won't do. Put it down and get it signed. Have the written words say what is to be done by and to who, when and how it is to be done, how much it's going to cost who, and who gets how much of the spoils.

Even a perfectly written contract can be gotten around by someone who wants to rip you off or weasel out of something. But getting things in writing minimizes risk, and spells out exactly what is expected.

A *contract* is a very definite legal sort of beast. It is an agreement between two parties to do or not do something in the future. What is to be done has to be legal and possible. Each side has to part with something of value, called a *consideration*.

Most importantly, there has to be a meeting of the minds. Contracts cannot legally be unconscionable, letting one side rip the other off.

Trouble is that it may take a bunch of effort and hassle to show what is unconscionable and what isn't.

Always think in terms of a written contract whenever you set something up that is going to cost you in the way of money, energy, or time. It's fine to be easy going and verbally agree to minor things most of the time. But, sometimes, who you are dealing with—that nice guy or gal over there—is blatantly out to do you in. Other times, the nice guy over there may not be in charge of others, particularly those holding onto the bag of nickels. Set yourself some limit, such as $200 in value or a day's not-for-fun time. Above this limit, get it written down. Always and without exception.

It's also real handy to be able to prove that things happened in the past. This is particularly important for taxes and real estate transactions. This means you should save all receipts of every expense you pick up, both in your money machine and outside of it. When and wherever possible, get written receipts or other records of what you have spent in the past. This will also prove real handy in case of a ripoff or an accident as well, and is essential if you are going to return something that turns out defective or otherwise ungood.

Get it on paper. And keep it.

unmatter—sign nothing major without cooling off

Another good idea is to age anything major overnight or longer before you sign it. While most states do have a law that lets you get out of many things three days or so after you sign, this isn't quite the same thing and should not be something you rely on.

There are several obvious reasons to wait. One is that you can back off and cool it and look at just what you are up to. A second is that you can check into options and talk to others for their opinions. The third is that you might have just been sold down the river and can still back out without any face saving.

An even better reason to age things overnight is that it gives you a good check on the reasonableness or honesty of the other side. If they try to talk you out of waiting, or give you all sorts of irresistible reasons why your signature is needed instantly, *run away*! Immediately. You have already been had. Cut your losses and run.

The thing to watch for is mild apprehension over your waiting. This is normal and often shows that you aren't being hit too bad. But, watch out for the yahoo who tells you six times over "absolutely—take it home, look it over, think it out, ask others," for this is almost a sure sign that you are being fed a snow job. Excessive reassurances are almost as good a ploy as an immediate closure—and can rip you off just as badly.

***unmatter—NEVER confront any government official on
any level at any time for any reason***

There is nothing more dangerous to your money machine than a
hacked off bureaucrat. This applies to anyone in any level of government. The dogcatcher, the clerk at the post office, the building inspector, the zoning people—all these can do you in just as badly and easily
as the more obvious bad guys can. Chances are the pettier the job, the
pettier the person behind it. Which, in turn, means the more time and
energy they can devote to giving you a rough time.

Once again, our magic words *low profile* crop up. If you aren't
going to get a dog license, don't let your dog run. Don't tell the building inspector you are going to violate the code. Or, get him on your
side somehow, maybe by sponsoring his racing team or supporting
another pet project of his. *Mordida* or *Bakeesh* needn't be in cash. Be
nice to the people at the post office. After all, it's a real challenge
damaging and slowing up all that mail. Don't tell zoning you have
a business in your home. But at the same time, don't be obvious
with a large sign, heavy traffic, or objectionable fumes, noises, or
appearance.

Keep cool. Be cool. Stay cool.

unmatter—don't mess with the eagle

The eagle is the feds. They have a very long memory, infinite megabucks, and all the time in the world to hassle you with. Forever and
ever. Now, it makes just plain common sense to not go burning
crosses on the CIA's front lawn. And groups like the FBI, the narcs,
and the IRS are obviously people you want to stay on the right side of.
Better yet, you want to avoid them entirely.

But there's lots of other groups out there that are just as happy to
give you a rough time. Let the FCC find out you've clipped a home-
built electronic game or computer onto the antenna terminals of a TV
set without paying the required $3100 type-approval fee for instance.
Or, ask someone with a bunch of employees about a friendly little
group called OSHA. And there's lots more where these came from.

I've seen several people into really good money machines blow
everything they have done by deciding a law is bad and then confronting the law and making an example of themselves. No way can you
win this game. The other side has all the cards, all the people, all the
time, a permanent memory, and all the nickels.

Never mess with the eagle. If you decide a law is ungood or doesn't
apply to you, be cool about it. Never advertise or flaunt an overlook-
ing or an outright breaking of the law. Never pick a law to break that

enough others already have broken to the point where the eagle has his attention gotten.

Leave those tailfeathers intact. They make lousy souvenirs.

unmatter—no lawyer, unless . . .

Lawyers are obviously expensive. Many of them have a habit of making the simple complex and muddying the water around an issue. They also have a way of introducing psychic energy sinks and mistrust into places where none existed before. Legal procedures are almost always extremely long and drawn out affairs. So, before you go to any lawyer, ask yourself if these disadvantages will outweigh any good a lawyer can do for you.

A good rule is to use a lawyer only when it is immediately obvious *to a disinterested outsider* that you will (1) immediately and certainly lose a bunch of money or time if you do not do so, and (2) there are extremely good odds that this loss can be dramatically reduced or minimized with good legal help.

Just because you are mad or have been ripped off, don't assume automatically that legal help will let you "get even". If you have been done in, it's often too late. Stirring things will only make matters worse. Write it off and start anew is often the best route. Remember that the other side may have a lawyer, too, doing everything he can to protect his client's best interests. If he can do nothing else, he should be able to drag things out forever and minimize any recovery you may eventually make.

Let's take an example. It is two years ago. I have just been ripped off to the tune of five kilobucks by a coin company that took the money and ran. I even had in writing the coin company admitting they took the money and ran. Even I was convinced that this was simple enough and direct enough that a lawyer could bail me out. So I got one. And a competent and reasonably priced one. After only a few months, the lawyer got a countersigned *and guaranteed* one year note.

One year later, of course, the note is defaulted. More legal action is taken. A judgment is served. It is now two years later and still no return, although inexorable legal progress is definitely being made. Legal fees have only been a few hundred dollars so far, but . . .

First, had I actually received this particular coin, it would have nearly doubled in value during this time. Had I just written the debt off immediately, around half of it would be "refunded" through business taxes not paid. But, by taking an obvious legal route in a cut and dried situation where it looks like legal help was the obvious way to go, I have neither coins, cash, nor writeoff, and am down several hundred bucks and two years time. No way can the time or the bad vibes be recovered.

A lawyer can be a good idea for a few limited times when bad vibes aren't normally involved. Having one help you with a will can be a good idea, particularly if you do not live in a community property state. Having one explain a complex contract to you might be a good idea. But, if the contract is that complicated, you shouldn't be there in the first place. Your money machine should keep things simple, straightforward, and easy to understand.

unmatters—third party all unpleasantries, . . .

Times are almost certain to crop up when somebody is going to be unhappy with something you have to do. Maybe a bill owed you is long overdue. Maybe you simply don't want to deal with someone, despite or even because of the pressure they are putting on you. Maybe you are getting badly ripped off and have to do something about it. Or, maybe you are simply being led somewhere you don't want to go. How do you handle these times?

One good route is called the *third party technique*. You simply exit stage left and let some third party clean up the mess.

Two examples:

* You sell a house you own outright and are willing to carry paper on it, but want to avoid the bad trip of having to collect the rent each month and the badder one of getting done in. Let a title company carry the credit and collection for you at a few dollars a year. Better yet, take the cash and buy something called a *Ginny Mae*, an investment into a government backed and guaranteed pool of other peoples' mortgages.

* Someone calls you and tries to get you to send a free preprint of your thousand page new book. You live in a town where xerox still costs a quarter a page, and no way do you feel that the preprint will ever return anything to you. Simply tell the someone that the publisher forbids it.

The trick to avoid any unpleasantries is to get yourself out of the spotlight and put something incredibly harder to argue with in your place. The absolutely ideal situation is to use *two* equally nebulous bureaucracies or granfalloons who can then blame each other and still be very hardnosed. You have just used a third party, or a pair of third parties, to bail you out.

This two-crossed-granfaloons route hit me wrong way around a while back, and makes an excellent, if painful, example of how well this works. A savings and loan stopped paying my house taxes for several years. Later I paid for the house and they closed out the account, not mentioning this fact. Later still, I sell the house, and the county suddenly demands $2000 in back taxes. Question: who do you go and beat up?

In simpler problems, just invent some unarguable, nebulous, and preferably nonexistent third party to get you off the hook. Some ferinstances:

* That's against company policy

* I'll have to check with accounting on that.

* I think it may be down at the other office

* Legal will type up some contingency fee liability release acceptance repudiation determent forms for you. Who are your attorneys?

* Delivery is running around 43 weeks right now. I might be able to pull some strings and shorten it to 39 weeks for you.

* What year were you originally expecting completion?

and, if all else fails . . .

* I'll have to refer it to the steering committee next time they meet.

But, please, please don't blame it on the poor computer. Any third party stunt at all but that.

. . . or use the DOT technique

Suppose you have a more minor hassle. You want to be totally honest, but simply want to stay away from something or stop something from happening or at least from happening right away. The DOT technique will bail you out of these dilemmas. DOT stands for

Dwell On Trivia

and gives you a handle on things like this. Simply pick nonessential but apparently important things to talk about. Worry about detail, nuance. More bluntly, stall and muddy the water.

In fact, the DOT idea is good enough that you should put a small dot near your telephone as a reminder of this valuable tool to keep you out of things you want to avoid.

One important point: Both third-partying and the DOT technique are *defensive* measures. You only use them when you want to specifically avoid something or keep something from happening. Under no circumstances should you use these as an aggressive or offensive way of handling your money machine matters.

unmatter—no patents

I very strongly feel that patents have no place whatsoever in a succesful money machine. Why? Here are some reasons for openers:

* A patent does not automatically mean that people will pay you for your invention. All it means is that you have the right to sue somebody. The ability to collect is something else entirely.

* Patents cost money and take a long time to get. In fast turnover fields like electronics or computers, it may take six years to get a patent on something that is going to be improved or outdated in six months. This borders on lunacy.

* There is a whole aura of paranoia and psychic energy sinks associated with the "stealing my secret" aspects of patenting.

* There is not one patent in a hundred that is profitable. There is not one patent in a thousand that cannot be thrown out or severely minimized following a diligent enough search for prior art in obscure enough places.

* Many granfalloon-type corporations would much rather give their legal department $100,000 to bust your patent before they would stoop to giving you $10,000 in royalties.

* If you ever do get a patent, anybody in the world can find out your key secrets by paying 50¢ for a copy of the patent.

and, last but not least . . .

* If you happen to *really* be the type of genius that is truly capable of inventing a new wheel and beating the one-in-a-thousand odds, the only way you could have gotten that way in the first place was by having a blind spot that ignores people and legal details. The history of many well-known patents bears this out.

A rather grim picture at best. Worse yet, a chase after non-existent megabucks combined with the paranoia of a psychic energy sink. Worst of all, time and effort blown that is better spent inventing new things or improving what you already have.

So, how do you treat your "patentable" ideas, and how do you react to somebody else who thinks you are violating *his* patent?

The best possible patent protection you can get is to publish your key secrets in a national magazine or other widely circulated journal. Be sure to show all key details, all trade secrets, and spell out all the disadvantages and limitations.

What does this do for you? Well,

* It generates an immediate hundred to a thousand dollars of cash through the article payment, putting you way ahead at the starting gate. Your idea is *already* profitable.

* It tucks the idea safely away in the public domain, preventing anyone else from patenting it.

* It gives you free advertising that will give you needed contacts and ways to sell and improve your products.

* It starts up the *Not Invented Here* syndrome that will set larger granfalloons to bad-mouthing what you did, rather than ripping the idea off.

* The time delay in publishing lets you automatically stay six months to a year ahead of everybody else working with the ideas.

If your idea is so good that you think it's "patentable," there will be lots more of them where it came from. Funnel your energy into developing and using the ideas, rather than the hassle and paranoia of trying to "protect" something you already have in a quest for nonexistent megabucks.

As a general rule, the more you feel your idea is worth "patenting," the more useless the idea really is. I've personally seen this time and time again in my consulting work. The more secretive the potential client is and the more certain he is of patentability, the more useless and worthless the thing he is working on.

Patently absurd, sort of.

Now, how about the other side of the coin? What do you do when someone hassles you about using *his* patent illegally? First, you ignore him. Never confront. Don't forget good old third partying and the DOT technique.

Secondly, recognize that you or anybody else has the right to build anything for themselves for their own intellectual curiosity, and a patent holder can't do anything to stop you. If your money machine is selling something that clearly violates a patent that you feel would cost you a bunch to bust, change over to offering kits of parts, detailed how-to instructions, raw materials, and so on. Let your clients in turn be the ones to violate the patent. Only those that build more than one will be in violation, and the patent holder now has all sorts of third parties to chase.

If all else fails, go find some prior art. Rarely will a large granfalloon hassle you over a patent. It doesn't look good for their "David-vs-Goliath" image, and attracts the attention of the antitrust people. Almost always, the yahoo who hassles you will have a very weak patent. I once was able to show prior art back to the seventeenth century to get a "new" color organ patent and patentee off my back. The crucial patent that outrageously priced ultrasonic Doppler burglar alarms for years and years was busted when   art was found in, of all places, Liechtenstein.

Two of the current patent paranoia trips involve using phase lock loop trackers in electronic music and ground compensation in metal detectors. Both of these have so much prior art involved that it is unbelievable these two dead horses are still being whipped.

Solar energy is another field mired in patent hassles.

Avoid the patent trip entirely.

unmatter—don't sweat copyright

What about copyright? This is another area where a lot of popular misinformation can cost you lots and lots of nickels. Any legitimate publisher will automatically copyright things for you in your name as they are published. There should be no charges or legal fees involved.

To prevent outright theft of unpublished stuff, there always has been *common law copyright* that says thou shalt not rip off someone else's material; recently this has become part of federal copyright law, giving you automatic protection. So, copyright is essentially free, first by federal law before publication, and then handled for you by whoever does the publishing. Even if you self-publish and register your own copyright, the total costs involved can be as low as $10.

Being free is about what a copyright is worth too. People often expect far too much from copyright. A copyright protects the exact *form* something appears in. It does not in any way protect the ideas or concepts behind that form, nor does it stop someone else from doing something parallel, sort of "alike but different somehow." While a copyright can prevent someone else from going out and printing 10,000 copies of your latest book, no way can it stop 10,000 people from each going out and Xeroxing one copy each of the same book or the key information in it.

The way around the copyright protection dilemma is to make your product so low in cost that no one can afford to duplicate it on their own in small quantities. A $4 to $9 technical paperback is unlikely to get widely copied. The same stuff in a $40 hardback book is almost certain to, particularly if it's required for a university course. A $5 cassette software program won't get ripped off because it takes more than $5 worth of hassle to duplicate a single copy. Charge $125, and you are bound to have some pirating. Besides, you probably will have less than 1/25th the number of customers at the higher price, even further cutting into your profits. Price your printed-circuit boards or other similar things below their cost of duplication in small quantities. This is the surest protection you can get.

Should you ever really want to copyright anything on your own, pick up details on how to do this from a nearby printer or publisher. Copyright protection is a simple and easy thing to get. It's also often a thing of little value to you.

unmatter—separate insurance protection from sucker bets

Have you ever looked at those fancy regional insurance centers with all those expensive buildings, sculpture, fancy fountains, and so on, and wondered just exactly where the money came from to pay for all of it? Or maybe you have been wondering why many insurance stocks and bonds are considered a good defensive buy and tend to do well regardless of what the economy is up to? Very simply, insurance is a business whose aim is to make money. They make their money by taking in more money than they give out, investing the difference in the best ways they can.

More money is taken in than is given out by taking as many sucker bets as possible. This is done by charging more than the reasonable odds of something, taking a profit out of it, and eventually paying off with highly inflated future dollars.

One key to your successful money machine is to not get taken in any sucker bets. *Some* insurance is *probably* needed. But, always ask yourself what you are getting and how much it is costing you. *Whenever and wherever possible, take as much of the risk you possibly can by yourself.* The whole idea of a money machine is to take risks to get a reward. Don't blow a lot of the return by paying others lots of money to minimize unlikely risks for you.

For instance, if you must own a car, a liability insurance policy is probably a good idea. If for no other reason, the hassle you have to go through without insurance isn't worth it in many states. But, do you really need collision insurance? Probably not, particularly with an older car. Recognize also that the type of vehicle you buy and how you claim you are going to use it also will dramatically change your insurance rates.

If you do use collision insurance, always take the maximum possible deductible with the fewest possible add-on options. Don't think of insurance as completely protecting you. Think of it as an emergency means of filling in only the worst part of anything bad that is reasonably likely to happen; absorb the rest yourself.

What about life insurance? **The HR-10 tax dodge of the next chapter gives you ABSOLUTELY FREE life insurance,** with no premiums, no exams, no contingencies, 100 percent cash value, and coverage increasing with the value of the trust as you get older.

A second and even better route to free life insurance was one of our key strategy secrets way back in chapter one—aiming for deferred income when and wherever possible. This gives you a continuing long term source of nickels not needing your immediate and continuous attention.

Should you have a heavy mortgage or other major financial burden, offset it with straight term life insurance. Straight term in limited amounts for short times may also be a good idea until the HR-10 value and the returns from your deferred income get big enough to take over.

As a general rule, the harder an agent tries to talk you out of a particular policy, the better a value it will be for you. This is especially true if the agent denies the existence of an obviously needed type of protection.

With your home and business insurance coverage, always take the maximum deductible and leave off the bells and whistles. Set the level of your coverage to absorb *only* the parts of a reasonably likely loss that you really couldn't absorb yourself if you had to.

One interesting trick is to hedge your insurance costs with some similarly yielding insurance stocks and bonds. This is another route to free insurance, although it does tie up some cash. This way, you recycle your insurance dollars and at the same time pick up some of the sucker bet winnings. Close the loop.

unmatter—stay out of local politics

Somewhere west of the Pecos, in a little desert town that shall remain nameless*, is a collection of some 500 pickup trucks, four-wheel drive vehicles, off-road bikes, sand rails, and even a few more or less ordinary cars. Of these 500 vehicles, 499 of them have at least one bumper sticker on them that says "SIERRA CLUB—HIKE STRAIGHT TO HELL."

The 500th vehicle, which happens to be a VW microbus, is owned by a Sierra Club member. He is a Sierra Club member because he is

---

*We won't even mention its 85344 zipcode.

one of those bugs-and-bunny environmental freaks that genuinely believes in the need for protection and restoration of the environment, and improvement of the quality of life.

He happens to be me. Or I, or whatever. Now, in a small town, everything is connected to everything else.

Is it ever.

And in ways that you seldom might suspect. If it weren't for the fact that the bumper sticker is a classic example of negative advertising that benefits the Sierra Club tremendously, I'd be hacked off at these people and wouldn't want to do business with them.

Now, from the local's point of view, they wouldn't mind if you were a horsethief, or even a lying, burro-shooting polecat. They *might* even be able to tolerate someone who put beans in his chili. But, a Sierra Club member is something that they just can't cope with. It simply cannot be. It just does not fit in. It won't compute.

What all this has to do with you is simply this: Whatever political position or stand you take on a high profile basis WILL alienate some of your customers and some of your suppliers. High profile politics, particularly local ones with people you have to continually work and live with, is an absolute no-no for your money machine. DO NOT involve yourself or your business. Politics is less than a zero sum game that cannot survive if enough accurate information flow exists. Spend the time on the information flow, and the need for any politics will go away.

If you really believe in something, *quietly* support it as strongly as you want to, but do it in a non-obvious way. Use your lifestyle as an example to others that you are practicing what you believe in.

This no-involvement stance also solves the dilemma of getting hit up for political support, especially from both sides of an issue at once. If you support nobody, it is an easy matter to tell anyone who hits you up this fact, and they may even believe you. At any rate, they will go away when they see you are serious.

If you think something is important, fine, go out and support it. But, don't do it in any way that will turn off your customers or suppliers, or in any way that can hurt the long-term prospects for your money machine.

unmatter—watch publicity

Know the difference between *advertising* and *publicity*. We'll call advertising the stuff you are in control of that will expose you and your money machine to more clients, sales, and *useful* contacts. Publicity is stuff done by others that serves other needs and that can backfire on you. Publicity can do you far more harm than good.

Keep your picture out of the local paper. Avoid statements to the press. Don't let your plans be known. Discourage others from writing about you, your lifestyle, or your business. Publicity of this type exposes you to many non-clients and other time and energy wasters. It can grossly magnify and misinterpret you. It can lead to a monumental psychic energy sink. It also sets you up for all sorts of potential ripoffs.

A minor point that goes along with all this—never confront a media freak head on. You can NEVER win confronting an author or an editor in his *own* paper or magazine. They *always* will have the last word in any media they control. Stay out of the letters columns. Do not rebut. Ignore them or they will make a fool out of you.

unmatter—use both jeweler's screwdrivers and sledgehammers

This unmatter is the one about crying wolf too often. Or ever. If you just once send a special delivery letter to every member of a granfallon's board of directors; you will most likely get immediate action beyond your wildest dreams. The second time you try it, they will begin to get suspicious, and the third time, you'll be branded a kook forever.

When you are trying to get something to happen, use just barely the amount of force that will be needed to definitely get results, and *apply that force at the lowest practical level and in the most inconspicuous way you can.* The trick is to do just enough to get results and do it only as often as is needed and no more. Then get off everyone's case. If you have to repeat things later on, vary your approach and try a different attack angle.

No matter what your money machine, if you get identified as a source of hassles, bad vibes, or continual bitching, it is bound to do you in one way or another. The less often you do something, the more will be its impact.

unmatter—a warning on working and living together

If you happen to like whoever you are living with and want them to be around for a while, do NOT—repeat—do NOT involve both of you in the same money machine on a full time, total lifestyle basis. Being around each other 18 hours a day may be nice and fine, but standing in each other's back pockets 24 hours a day forever and ever won't hack it. Don't try it. Don't even think about it.

Teamwork is fine. Complementary skills are a very good thing for a money machine and can be almost essential. But, if you want you, your relationship, and your money machine to go for the long haul, do it this way instead:

* Have one of you be the 100% full time honcho of a particular money machine. Let the other be a part time honchee, or helper.

* Make sure the honchee has a totally separate source of nickels that needs no accounting for and is in no way involved with the money machine. The amount needn't be a great heaping bunch, but it absolutely has to be more than an "allowance."

* Make sure the honchee has their own money machine or other means of creative expression.

* Be certain that both of you have separate places to hide and separate means of escape. Neither of you should need any excuse or justification to do either.

* Thou shalt never compete directly against each other, hassle each other, or do the same type of thing for the money machine.

* Take separate vacations or otherwise get away from each other a significant percentage of the time.

* Agree *exactly* on the openness of your lifestyle.

I've just seen two really good money machines fall apart because these survival guidelines were ignored. In one case, an outstanding computer art money machine was scuttled by being together too much and a large difference in opinion as to how open the lifestyle should be. In a second, a specialty restaurant, and incidentally the best one for miles and miles around, got into deep trouble because the honchee wanted some money to spend on her own and some time for her own use.

In my own money machine, I am the honcho, and Bee is the honchee. She does all the accounting, taxes, paper shuffling, proofing, and people hassling when it is needed. But, she has her own separate money machines that include teaching, weaving and crafts, photography and travel stories, and museum work. Cash from these is totally separate from the main trip and is used anyway she wants. Her escapes include crawling-on-the-grass books and hiding in the little house we rented down the street. Mine include the fire department and spelunking. We often spend summers with the Forest Service, sometimes on separate ranger districts, but always apart for long stretches at a time.

In your own money machine, always remember that too much of anything is bad, no matter how good it seems at the time. If anyone ever feels trapped or stomped on, you are in deep trouble. Plan for survival. Survival for you, your money machine, and your relationship.

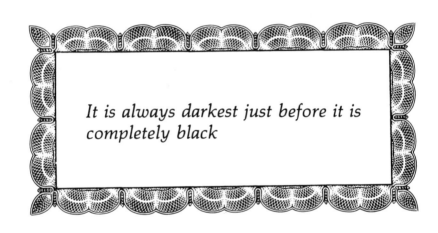

It is always darkest just before it is completely black

EIGHT

Tax Dodges

One of the really neat things you get to do when you have a winning money machine is pay great heaping gobs of taxes. Since you are doing things on your own, you'll even get to pay your taxes *quarterly* instead of only once a year. Good old form 1040-ES. And, just wait till you see what your "fair share" of that big old chain letter in the sky— social security—is. Why, you're so lucky you get to pay much more than you used to pay working for someone else. And with zero hope of ever getting more than a tiny percentage of it back.

Now, some people might argue that taxes serve a useful purpose. After all, things like supersonic pork barrels, the nuclear travesty, and chess games with KGB cost money. The ideal thing would be to have the people that think these things are important pay for them out of their own pockets, but till then, you're stuck with a bunch of the load.

Somewhere there has to be a way to minimize all this. Or at least your share of it. We'll ignore the obvious of simply not reporting income, moving outside the country, or otherwise fudging. First, because this violates our important don't-mess-with-the-eagle unmatter. But, more importantly, with some creative time and effort, you can often minimize your taxes much more certainly, lots more in amount, and much more legally than you can by simply cheating and then worrying about it. In fact, it turns out that your money machine offers lots of unique opportunities to minimize your tax bite. The trick, of course, is tuning yourself into them.

We'll call a *tax dodge* anything that minimizes the time, hassle, or money spent on taxes. Very fortunately, the tax law *expects* you to aggressively minimize your tax bill. The only gotcha is that it has to be done within legal or at least reasonably arguable guidelines. Let's look at some possible tax dodges for your money machine. Then, we'll turn to the ultimate tax dodge secret that lets you get as much of your tax money back from the feds as you like.

tax dodge— having a money machine in the first place

A business-type money machine puts you in the nice position to be able to itemize deductions *and* take a standard deduction at the same time. With very few exceptions, anything that is an expense to your money machine is tax deductible and removable from your income. All your materials costs, utilities, rent, operating expenses, postage, business contributions, and so on are subtracted from your gross before any taxes are computed. Now with a little creative and totally legal effort on your own, you can derive pleasure and enjoyment from these expenses even while they are serving a legitimate business purpose.

What *isn't* immediately deductible?

* **Things that will be around for a while, like machinery.** You can deduct machinery, but you have to *depreciate* your deduction over the useful life of the machine.

* **Anything that increases the value of something physical.** Anything that goes into a building or another *capital* increasing purpose isn't deductible. For instance, a $2000 overhaul of an air conditioner is deductible as a maintenance expense, but adding a $200 cooler to a previously uncooled building is not. When the building or whatever is sold later, the capital improvements are recovered as expenses.

* **Illegal losses in excess of illegal gains**. You are only allowed to deduct gambling losses or a dope burn to the extent that you also declare income from these activities.

* **Stunts that others have abused**. There has been so much flagrant violation of the travel and entertainment expenses, as well as home office deductions that *very* restrictive rules must be *exactly* followed if you are to tap these as deductions. For instance, travel must be overnight, primarily for an obvious business purpose, and a log must be kept. For a home office deduction, the *entire* room or rooms have to be used *exclusively* as your *main* place of business, and so on.

What can you write off? Ask yourself this anytime you spend money on anything. How about a bag of Purina Doggy Chow? If you are

130

running a kennel, certainly. If you have a guard dog, certainly. If you have a dog who is genuinely useful as a watch dog for your money machine but is also the family hound, probably half the bag can be deducted. If you only have a loveable mutt or an ole yeller dawg, forget it.

How about a caving trip? If the trip is for a scientific and non-profit purpose and has an obvious sponsor, you can usually write off your expenses but not your time. The same goes if it is a major conservation effort or cleanup in cooperation with a government agency. If you're just going to go out and crawl around underground and get muddy, forget most of the writeoff. But, you can still deduct your hard hat since it is safety equipment.

Whenever you spend money on anything, ALWAYS seek a legitimate business purpose that lets you remove this money from your income before taxes. If you can write it off, write if off. If you can depreciate it, depreciate it. If you can capitalize it, capitalize it. If you can't think of anything that works, avoid spending the money.

One obvious question. What is a business and what is a hobby? To the IRS, a business has a genuine intent to make money. Normally, they want to see your money machine showing a profit two years out of five. There are a few lifestyle exceptions to this rule, such as if your Daddy was a farmer, you are a farmer, you look like a farmer, you act like a farmer, and you smell like a farmer. The feds tend to get very suspicious if you exceed this two-of-five rule and just won't go along with your forever losing money on your model railroad.

tax dodge—accurate records

There are all sorts of nuances and subtleties in the tax law. So many, in fact, that granfalloon corporations and the very rich can use all sorts of creative stunts to avoid paying taxes. It turns out that so long as you have an accounting method (no matter how lenient or absurd), and it looks like you *strictly* and *meticulously* followed it, at worst, the feds can eventually make you pay some back taxes, if and when they get around to hassling you over it.

On the other hand, if you can't show how you've done something or it looks like you simply ignored taxes, this is fraud and a no-no. Fraud, of course, comes complete with criminal penalties and other assorted nastiness.

So, **SAVE ALL EXPENSE RECORDS FOREVER.** Some examples of things to save:

* All receipts of everything you buy. Get receipts and be able to prove purchase even if a hassle is involved.

* On trips and travel, save all receipts, plus keep an *up-to-date* log that shows where you went, when you went, why you went, what was gained, the business purposes of the trip, and how much it cost.

* On any real estate transaction, keep track of *all* expenses. This applies to your house as well as any business property. Anything you can show as an expense gets capitalized and comes off any profit (or adds to the loss) when you sell.

* Be able to show where the money went. Show that materials were in fact used up, worn out, delivered, shipped, or donated. Buying things, writing them off and then reselling them at a yard sale for undisclosed cash is a no-no. You can get away with a little of this, but not very much. The more accurate your records of everything else, the more of this you can get away with.

* Be able to show *exactly* how you keep your records. The type of bookkeeping in use, the way you calculate depreciation, the methods of accounting, your tax basis, and so on.

The more accurate and the more completely you keep your records, the less basis there is for any arguments with the feds, and the less likely they are to hassle you. It's extremely important to keep your records up to date. Tax accounting should be a *continuous* activity, not some panic-mode thing that happens once a quarter or once a year.

Keep everything forever.

tax dodges—off-the-top bookkeeping . . .

This is a trick that gets you to pay your taxes, retirement, and other fixed expenses *first* before you do anything dumb with the money. Its main uses are to give you a more realistic picture of where you are financially at any particular instant and to eliminate crisis-mode operation at tax time.

To use off-the-top bookkeeping, every time you get a major check or other money machine payment, take 30 percent of it and *immediately* set it aside for taxes. Take 10 percent and *immediately* set it aside for retirement. Take 5 percent and *immediately* set it aside for other fixed expenses. Adjust the percentages to suit your own shade of reality.

Only the money left is to be entered into your working balance for your money machine. You can actually set up separate accounts or simply list things under separate columns. If you get heavy into lots of nickels, then the tax and retirement funds can go into T-bills, a savings account, or some other short-term "investment," up till quarterly tax time rolls around.

For this to work for you, you must keep your cotton picking paws off the tax and retirement funds at all times, even if this puts your apparent working balance deep into the red.

Just changing some numbers around won't, of course, alter how much comes in the door or goes out as taxes. But it will give you a much clearer picture of what you have to work with at all times. It also eliminates the bad vibes of a sudden bill becoming immediately due with no way to pay it.

At the end of every tax year, adjust how much is left over or needed for taxes and retirement to match your expected income. Obviously, if tax funds are left over after all taxes are paid, use them elsewhere and reduce your "witholding."

. . . and the steam calliope fund

This is another "slice it differently" trick that may help you keep things in order. It is a super simple mode of zero-interest forced savings that might be a good idea for a starting money machine. The steam calliope fund is aimed at building up a small fund that covers you for unexpected arithmetic errors, sudden small expenses, minimum checking balances, tax surprises, and so on.

To start your fund, just round off all your bank deposits to the nearest five or ten dollars. The excess goes into the calliope fund and continues to build up, an average of a few dollars per deposit.

Once your bookkeeping is up and you are no longer making stupid mistakes, the fund will start to accumulate. You can drop it once you actually have enough money in it to go out and buy a steam calliope.

tax dodge—depreciation

The tax law says that if something is going to be around for a while, you can only write off a portion of it each year of its useful life. Thus, for machinery, equipment, office furniture, computers, and so on, you aren't allowed to simply write off the cost of the beast when you buy it. Instead, you have to calculate the useful life of the machine, subtract its salvage value, and then write off only so much each year. This is called *depreciation*.

The bad thing about depreciation is that you have to do it in the first place, instead of just writing things off. There are several good things about it:

* Eventually you do indeed write off something just as if it were a current business expense.

* You can write things off somewhat faster than they are really "used up" and pretty much stay ahead of the game.

* After you have been depreciating things for a few years, a big pack of old things still getting written off automatically comes off the top of your gross before any taxes are computed.

* Writing things off faster than they are used up in effect gives you a free long-term loan from the feds you can use any way you like.

Since the exact rules keep changing, check into current IRS booklets for the exact details on depreciation. You are allowed to write things off faster than the obvious *straight line* method, up to and including a method called *double declining balance*. One simple accelerated depreciation method is to write off 20% immediately and then use straight line for what is left over.

For instance, on a $1000 printing press with an 8-year life and zero salvage value, you write off $200 + $100 = $300 the first year, and $100 each additional year.

The advantage of fast depreciation is that you are writing off things before you are using them up, in effect getting a free loan from the feds. The free loan looks even better during high inflation times. A minor disadvantage of the fast writeoff methods is that there is a bunch of bookkeeping involved. Thanks to today's home computers, this is no longer a big deal.

But, there is one thing that can get very sticky with fast writeoffs. If you use fast depreciation, you have to "recapture" back to straight line if you sell out. Otherwise the feds end up taxing you at a capital-gains rate for free money they gave you in the first place. This bends them out of shape in the worst way. Recapture paperwork and calculations are horrendous, but are probably worth the effort if you sell out of something expensive before it is fully depreciated.

What about automobiles? You can depreciate any portion of a car, truck, or other vehicle used for business purposes. But, it's often much simpler and more profitable to take a mileage allowance of so many cents a mile instead. You should compare both methods and pick the best one for you. If you are into older vehicles, lower cost ones, and ones with good fuel economy, you are usually better off taking straight mileage. Straight mileage will usually benefit you if the car is used both for business and pleasure.

Depreciation can be a particularly good deal in apartments and other real estate rentals.

tax dodge—investment tax credit

Here is a super tax deal. In order to keep the gross in the gross national product, the feds decided that business needs an incentive to keep buying the production stuff needed to expand the economy. So, an *investment tax credit* is available on pretty much everything you depreciate. At this writing, this credit is ten percent.

For instance, if you buy a $1000 printing press, *besides* the depreciation, an *additional* $100 can be *immediately* deducted from your *present* tax bill.

In one particular money machine I know of that involved a print shop, the honcho was able to buy so much printing equipment that he totally eliminated *all* taxes he *ever* previously paid, thanks to his investment tax credits.

For full credit, the beast you buy has to have a useful life over seven years. Up to three years, you get nothing. You get one-third as much for three to five years, and two-thirds as much for a five to seven year useful life.

You can get the credit on an automobile, but only on the percentage you use for business, and only the fraction based on how long you keep the car. For instance, on a $3600 pickup truck used three years, half for business, you get a tax credit of one-sixth the usual 10%, or only $60. Still, it's a thing to nail down. You can take this credit, even if you use mileage instead of depreciation.

Investment tax credit is one of the few all-around good tax deals for your money machine. Of course, it's an outright ripoff for people *without* money machines, but that's their problem. There is a possibility that investment tax credit may be extended to include structures and buildings in the future. This may be an even better deal, so watch for it if it happens.

tax dodge—know the difference between absolute and incremental tax rates

The value of a money machine dollar changes radically, depending on whether it is the *first* one or the *last* one you earn in a particular year. Knowing the difference can dramatically change how you spend your money, how much things cost you, and your whole outlook on taxes.

Your *absolute* tax rate is based on taking the amount of tax you paid, and dividing it by your total amount of taxable income. This will be around 25 to 30 percent for a successful money machine.

Your *incremental* tax rate is the tax you pay on every excess dollar you earn. This rate is the sum of the final "plus _____% above $X000" rates of your state and federal returns, with a few extra percent thrown in for social security, inflation, and other hidden taxes. It can easily go well over 50% for your money machine, even if it is only mildly a winner.

There are lots of ways to use your awareness to this crucial difference between average and incremental tax dollars:

* An extra dollar unspent is the equivalent of *two* you don't have to earn.

* An extra dollar spent on some business purpose gets combined with a free dollar from the feds letting you buy twice as much.

* An extra dollar donated to a worthy and tax deductible cause gets matched with a free dollar from the feds.

* Time spent proving extra dollars are really deductible pays you one dollar for every two you can write off. The per-hour pay can be much greater than any other money machine activity.

This awareness is sort of like welfare for the rich. Here is one example of how to use your awareness of the difference between the first and last earned dollar:

Suppose you kinda halfway need a drill press that is on sale at $100. How much is it going to cost you?

Now, if you do NOT have a money machine, the price of the drill press will be around $105, including the sales tax. If you are in an 50% incremental tax bracket, with no money machine, you'll have to earn $210 to pay for the press. Kinda bad.

But, if you *do* have a money machine, the drill press still costs around $100. You can eliminate the extra five bucks with a tax stamp. But, since your drill press is a legitimate business expense, you only need earn $100 to pay for it.

But wait, there's more to come. Good old investment tax credit. You get another $10 knocked off your tax bill for helping the drill press company keep the national product gross. Ten bucks off taxes is the equivalent of twenty you didn't have to earn, so knock this twenty off the drill press price. You have just bought a drill press for $80. The epsilon minus down the street just spent $210 for the same thing.

Pay very careful attention to your incremental dollars on top of the heap. Any workable way you can think of that keeps the feds' till-tapping fingers off these excess dollars will pay you very handsomely for your effort.

tax dodge—an HR-10 retirement fund

An HR-10 is also known as a *Keough Plan*. It's a retirement fund you can buy into. Money that goes into the fund comes off the top of your income before taxes are computed. However, later when you draw from the fund, you are taxed both on the amount you put in and the earnings. So, this is *not* a tax-free investment, but simply a good way to defer taxes for a very long time.

You can set aside 15% of your money machine income up to a $7500 yearly limit, provided you are in no other retirement plan. The plan must be approved by the IRS. You can get one at a full service bank or through some other financial institutions. It pays to shop around since the conservativeness of the investment and the stuff invested in changes from plan to plan.

The advantages of an HR-10 are:

* It immediately takes bunches off the top of your income before taxes are computed.
* It is a forced method of retirement savings
* You get free life insurance through a designated beneficiary.
* You may end up paying the deferred taxes in a much lower bracket.

And, on the bad news side:

* The money is permanantly locked in till you are of retirement age.
* The money is "professionally" managed, which means it will have trouble fighting inflation or increasing significantly in value.
* If you have long-term employees, you must share your fund with them, giving them equal benefits and opportunities to invest with you.
* A fixed, minimum management fee in the early years can be steep, maybe $400 per year or more.

All in all, the HR-10 is a reasonably good deal, especially if you contribute the limit each year and have no employees. It's extremely important to contribute as much as you can during the early years to get the minimum fees in line with something you can tolerate. You can contribute as much or as little as you like, up to tax time of the next year. Often you may have a choice of funds, perhaps being able to call out how much is to go into an equity (stock) fund or a fixed income (bond) fund. With some careful shuffling, you might be able to beat the long-term inflation odds.

sort of a tax dodge—the IRA

An IRA or *Individual Retirement Account* sounds almost as good as an HR-10. In reality, it's simply a stunt to keep people from taking their money out of a bank or savings and loan and putting it somewhere it can decently fight inflation and taxes.

IRA's are available to people working for others if they have no other pension plan. The IRA is limited to $1500 or so yearly maximum, which is not nearly enough to ever build up a useful retirement fund, particularly with accounts that are indexed to always yield below the inflation rate.

Still, an IRA does give you a way to take some cash off the top of your earnings before they are taxed, provided you can't tap the much better HR-10. But, don't think of it as anything individual, for retirement, or as an account. It's not.

tax dodge—income averaging

Income averaging lets you combine high and low income years and pay a tax based on the average of those years. Since the average is usually in a lower tax bracket than the peak, you can often benefit.

Unfortunately, you really have to make a killing in one year to benefit from averaging. Students in school are specifically excluded from averaging. Sorry about that.

You are allowed to average if your present income is $3001 more than 20% above the average for the last four years. How's that again? For instance, you can average if:

Average of last four year's income	This year's income
$5,000	$9,001
$10,000	$15,001
$25,000	$33,001
$100,000	$123,001

Just being able to average doesn't buy you anything. Your actual breakeven may be well above these values. It's only when you earn a *lot* more than the allowable amount each year that you can benefit a bunch by averaging.

Averaging is handy for authors and people in real estate where they may suddenly make a bunch of money in one year and little or nothing in other years.

You can average over and over again, every time you qualify. Generally, if your present income is sharply up, check into averaging. The paperwork takes fifteen minutes and is done after most other tax work. Chances are averaging won't do you a whole bunch of good, but it can definitely be worth checking into.

some mini-dodges

Here's a quick rundown of lots of tax dodges that can be very profitable for you:

* **Accurate information.** Any regional tax center has lots and lots of booklets and forms available. Collect them all. The IRS people will also answer your questions, but don't bug them in January or April. Get the better tax guides as well. Lasser's *Your Income Tax* has an index in it that alone is worth the price just as a checklist to see what you have forgotten.

* **Contributions.** Donate your leftover and otherwise out-of-date stock to schools and your old books and magazines to libraries and hospital auxiliaries. Anything else goes to a church rummage sale. Get receipts for the fair value of the stuff and deduct as a business expense.

* **Professional memberships.** Anything that is reasonably related to your business is a deductible expense. If you write hobby electronics stuff, all the hobby electronics magazines you buy are deductible, and so on.

* **The value of tax time.** Time spent doing your taxes can earn you hundreds or even thousands of dollars per hour. Spread this time out into a continuous and even-tempered process. Don't simply run panic mode for a few hours at the end of the year. It will cost you dearly.

* **Do your own taxes.** Do not seek out professional help. They will miss out on the things you can most effectively tap every time. They also are working for a few dollars, while you are working for many dollars on the same task.

* **Zero deductions.** If you take any temporary employment, claim zero deductions to prepay as much social security and taxes as you can. It will save hassle later on.

* **Family trusts.** Shifting income to a husband, a wife, or children can be a good deal since they might be in lower income brackets.

But there are all sorts of very sticky rules. Investigate carefully and then see what you can use.

* **Gifts.** You can transfer a gift to your children or others up to $3000 per year, or $60,000 total without paying any gift taxes. If these gifts are stock or other income producing investments, the money stays in the family and generates more nickels for you.

* **Pick the right state and the right town.** State and local wage taxes vary wildly as do their interpretation of who pays what. One author I know left Albuquerque because they were interpreting their inventory tax to include an author's uncompleted writings.

* **Bad debts.** These can be written off if they are legal looking enough and you take reasonable steps to get your money back. Only $2000 more in debts can be written off than you make in capital gains in a particular year. The rest can be carried forward.

* **Child care.** Nursery and baby sitting expenses while you are working are allowable, up to a possible $200 yearly tax credit.

* **Scientific expeditions.** Most often, you can deduct your expenses but not your time on a non-profit, conservation oriented, or scholarly venture.

* **Energy credits.** You can get a tax credit up to several thousand dollars a year on improvements that use renewable energy (like a solar panel) or that save energy (such as insulation). These credits are *in addition* to the normal capitalization or depreciation as a business expense.

* **Capital gains.** Long-term capital gains are (at this writing) taxed at a 30% rate. They are thus a very good deal to seek. Assets now have to be held at least one year.

tax dodge . . . watch out for catch 22

There is one little thing about tax dodges that you have to watch for very carefully. A tax dodge can have any use or purpose you like, except for one:

A tax dodge is not allowed to be a tax dodge.

For instance, you can start up a church because you believe in something. It can be the absolutely kookiest church in the world with the most ridiculous purposes. The only purpose that is not allowed is that the church be set up specifically as a tax dodge.

The same goes for everything else you can think of—museums, cattle, oil wells, off-shore games, movies, apartments, whatever. It is all right to use these things as tax dodges, but they must have some immediately obvious, defensible, and presumably more noble purpose than saving tax money.

Make sure all your tax dodges have completely obvious and legitimate purposes supporting them.

the ULTIMATE tax dodge—close the loop

One of the best kept secrets around is that you can get all of your income tax payments back anytime you like. You can even get much more in payments back than you ever made. This is how people get rich.

The dumb thing people do is apply to the IRS for their tax refund. The IRS is very uptight over refunding your money. But, **any other government agency** will gladly refund your tax money. All you have to do is politely ask them in a nice way at the right time.

Simply arrange to receive money from other government agencies. Ideally, you set the amount you receive to just barely exceed your tax bill. This is called *closing the loop*, or simply recycling your tax dollars.

For instance, you spend your summer vacation with the park service as a guide, with the forest service as a tree thinner, or even caving for the bureau of land management. Now, you write a check and give it to the IRS in April; they hand the check to the other agency in May; who in turn gives it back to you in June. That simple.

Or, you might qualify for research grants or tap other slush funds. Or simply teach at a public school or state university. Ask yourself what the feds blow their money on and get in line with the others.

But. Whoa. Isn't the pay for, say an assistant tree thinner rather dismal, and isn't it a lot of hard work, and aren't you really just trading time for tax dollars, sort of like going to jail for a while?

Well, not really.

First off, if you even think of your time spent as tax labor instead of a vacation and a break in your lifestyle, you are at least seeing *exactly* what purpose your equivalent tax dollars are going into. You are keeping those equivalent dollars out of the hands of people who will blow them on things you don't like or care for.

Even nicer, if your close-the-loop game can qualify as temporary employment, *and* if it is away from your money machine, *and* if your money machine continues on at the same address, *and* if what you are up to doesn't look like recurrent seasonal employment—get this—all of your food, travel, and lodging expenses during the entire job are tax deductible!

Which isn't bad at all. Now, if you know the job has to end and you have to be laid off without it being your own fault—such as at the end of tourist season or the end of fire season, you might even be able to qualify for unemployment and food stamps.

This could get tricky if you are the honcho of a $100,000-per-year money machine, but your honchee may be totally free to collect unemployment from the time he/she is laid off till the time to start back into teaching or whatever. No way will they get any job offers for the thing they were just laid off from since the season is over. Particularly a tree thinner living in the middle of the desert.

Keep all this a game. Stay strictly and absolutely within the letter of the law. Needless to say, you never tell anyone you are doing this to recycle your tax dollars. You shouldn't feel bad about this, since you are simply unripping some nickels the feds have ripped off from you. The feds don't feel bad about it, so why should you?

Now, the *exact* way you do this will depend on your own lifestyle. If you can't think of any other approach, just list everything the feds spend money for, and get on the list. It's obviously of great importance for this method to work that each and every one of you find your own individual and different way of tapping the till.

Close that loop, And keep it closed. Take your turn at the trough.

NINE

"Investments"

Eventually, when your money machine makes you filthy rich, you'll have piles and piles of money streaming in. You may have wondered just how to handle this problem. Simply letting the stuff pile up in the front yard usually isn't the best overall solution. Beside it being an obvious fire hazard, this violates our low-profile principle and may even invite ripoffs.

In theory, an "investment" lets you put this excess money somewhere to gain more money. A working "investment" is an ideal deferred income product, if it is capable of reliably returning extra dollars with little or no effort by you. Unfortunately, we have to put the word "investment" in quotes because

with one exception, there is no such thing as a good "investment."

Should a good, reliable and legal way to make lots of money ever be found, it will immediately be taxed, commissioned, inflated, odd-lotted, pointed, bid-asked differentialed, title insured, closing costed, restricted, termite sprayed and otherwise stomped upon to make it as bad as all the rest.

We might call a good investment something that reliably doubles its value in ten years. The quotes are there because you can't get there from here. At least not without a lot of luck, risk, and effort on your own.

Two examples drive this home:

A. To let the magic of compound interest work for you, you put $1000 in a 5% passbook savings account and let it sit for twenty years. What is your profit?

B. To make a quick buck on the stock market, you go to a name-brand broker and buy 100 shares of an OTC stock at 7½ Bid. Two weeks later, the stock goes up to 8½ and you sell. What is your profit?

The answer, of course, to both examples, is that your profit is zero. Your loss in case A is around $628. Your loss in case B is only $26, but you've blown the money 520 times as fast.

For the compound interest example, let's assume your de-facto incremental tax rate is only 50%, and that, by some miracle, inflation can be held to only a 7½ percent average over the next twenty years. Well, let's see. Each year, you earn 2½ percent on your account since half of the interest is taxed as ordinary income. This chops your personal inflation rate to a mere 5 percent a year, which drops the purchasing power of your $1000 to $372 in twenty years, leaving you with a net loss of $628.

On the stock transaction, since you bought OTC, the bid-ask differential was probably around half a point, meaning you buy a stock selling at 7½ bid at an ask price of 8. The one-way commission with a name brand broker will be around $38. So, your buy price is $838 and you sell at 850 minus another $38 commission, or at $812. Your net loss is $26.

Interestingly enough, the stock loss is your own dumb fault. Now, if you had bought an ASE or a NY stock at 7½ or an OTC stock with a price of 7½ Ask; and if you had gone to a discount broker rather than a ripoff broker; and if you had bought 400 shares at once instead of just 100, your profit would be around $81.50 per hundred shares.

Now, if you pull a deal like this over and over again for the same twenty years you did with the savings account, your final gross profit would be $35,305,200,000,000,000,000,000.00 per dollar invested. Taxes and inflation will reduce this to around $103,744,000,000.00, assuming you stay in a 50% bracket, and pay your tax as it is earned.

The gotcha is that you aren't likely to repeat this good a deal in today's stock market 520 times over without taking some risk. Nonetheless, our example does drive home the power of compound interest, when it is in fact working for you and when the compounding time is very short.

On any "investment", the key question is to ask yourself "Are there any odds at all of breaking even?". The usual answer is "No Way." At least not without a bunch of luck.

With this dismal conclusion in mind, let's at least see what is involved in minimizing the ripoffs that go with "investments" so that maybe you will have a fighting chance of at least deferring some nickels to enjoy later.

. . . that exception is your own money machine.

Remember way back when that our goal in a secret money mac.
is to get a 200 percent return on cash flow? We do this by combining
lots of personal value added to a minimum amount of cash flow, and
by keeping the scale of our money machine small enough that the
inefficiencies and communications problems of larger businesses don't
apply to us.

So, it's a relatively easy matter to do twenty times better on investment return than it is with most traditional "investments." Our obvious
rule should be **invest in yourself first.**

Wherever and whenever possible, plow excess funds back into your
own money machine and your own education. This does lots of good
things for you:

* No tax is paid on most money plowed back into the business.

* If the money plowed back goes into increasing productivity, the
   investment is also pretty much inflation proof.

* You have the ultimate in insider information to work with.

* You pay yourself all the commissions, odd lot differentials, points,
   and so on that others would try to tap from you.

There is a limit to all this. For each and every money machine, there
is an optimum size that maximizes your percentage return on cash flow
for a given amount of personal value added. What I've tried to show
you throughout this book is that the optimum business size is vastly
smaller (and incredibly more profitable) than the traditional rules
suggest.

So, always invest in yourself first, unless you get to the point where
dumping more cash into your money machine will clog the gears and
lower your percentage return.

Beyond this, blow some of your investment cash into having fun. It
keeps your head in the right place. But always use the powerful lever-
age of having-others-pay-you-for-your-fun to compound what you get
back on bucks spent.

"Investments"—if it seeks you out, it is NOT an investment

Anything that is heavily advertised or comes along with a super
salesman that makes money based on how much he sells you is NOT
an investment. It is an outright ripoff. Real estate land swindles, large
newspaper ads, those big "free toaster" ads in bank windows, flag-

waving buy-savings-bonds propaganda, things like this are not investments for you. They are simply ways for others to rip you off.

A workable "investment" for you *always* takes aggressive seeking-out on your own. Be very suspicious of any ad or any sales approach that wants your money. Decent "investments," and more importantly, the crucial timing for profits on any "investment," is something that is almost always kept quiet.

A corollary to all this is that anytime an "investment" hits the headlines, it is far too late to take any advantage of it. "Gold hits new high," or "Orange County real estate—the sky is the limit," or "Dow hits 1500!" may be what the news says. What the news means is that the horse is gone and the barn has burned down. Once the news is out, the game is over.

Except for the sucker bets.

It's the quiet times to watch for. Buy gold when everyone is laughing at those doomsaying gold bugs. Buy bonds when interest rates skyrocket out of sight. Buy stocks when the bottom is falling out of the market. As a good rule, invest in the *exact opposite* of what is grabbing the headlines at any particular time. When the big ole pendulum swings back, you'll be all set.

all "investments" are cyclical

There is no such thing as a "one decision" investment, something you continuously put money into that in turn gives you more money back. All "investments" have seasons in which they do very well, and times in which they do very bad. *Most popular "investments" will average their long-term return to zero or slightly less because of this cyclicity.* For instance, if you hold onto a stock long enough, its value is almost certain to drop below what you paid for it. If you buy a bond, times are almost certain to arrive when inflation unyields faster than the bond yields.

The obvious thing to do is buy in at the bottom of a cycle and sell out at the top. This gets tricky.

But the tricky part is NOT seeing into the future. Simply assuming that things will be cyclical in the future just like they have been in the past takes care of most of the clairvoyance for you. The tricky part is being able and willing to switch back and forth between "investments" so you can make the most of a particular economic situation. It takes raw guts to jump out of something that is doing fantastically good and switch over to something that is an obvious loser.

Here's how some of the more popular "investments" often react to cycles:

146

* **Bonds** are a very good buy during times of skyrocketing inflation and super high interest rates. Having a 12% bond during 7% inflation years is a good deal, particularly since you can easily sell it for much more than you paid for it. Having an old 2 or 3% bond during double-digit inflation is super bad, since it doesn't yield enough and can only be sold at a staggering discount.

* **Gold** does best when disaster strikes, particularly depressions, recessions, and galloping inflation. It is a very poor performer during times when things are stable and profitable, and during times when the biggies dump gold to shove the price straight down.

* **Stocks** are a good buy when the market is low and the business outlook poor, since the dividend yields are high and the price-earnings ratios are very low.

* **Real Estate** is closely tied to local economic conditions. People out of jobs rarely move or decide to add a vacation home. Too many people in an area destroy the original desirability of that area, through pollution, crime, traffic, higher taxes, double session schools, and so on. "Rent-vs-Buy" decisions are also keyed to the local economy.

* **Treasury Bills** and other short-term paper are a fairly reliable way to get just barely enough interest to stay ahead of inflation. It's often the best place to be if nothing better happens to be available at a particular time.

* **Commodities** are strictly a crap game with a stacked deck, besides being tied into climate, world economics, and insider manipulations. But—you want cycles, you've got them with commodities.

* **Collectibles** like art, stamps, coins, old cars, and so on tend to do very well during prosperity times but are *very* unliquid and lose value catastrophically during poorer times. They are also highly sensitive to popularity and mood.

So, make these cycles work for you. Pick several "investment" forms that suit you and be ready and able to switch back and forth as needed, compounding and pyramiding as you go along.

match "investments" to your lifestyle

You have to define and know exactly what you want to get out of an "investment." If keeping what you have is of utmost importance, then much more conservative "investments" are called for. If doing something with excess cash is more your game, then putting up the nickels for higher returns at higher risks is often the best choice.

Even more important, you have to key your "investment" program to your lifestyle. Some people like the excitement of short-term stock trading. Others can't stand the stress of sudden changes in value. People who dig fast action don't have the patience to wait out slower responding things like bonds. If you like dealing one-on-one with people, then real estate rentals and sales may be just for you. If you are a loner, pick something where a few words on paper or over the phone complete your transactions for you.

You might like to collect and display your wealth, such as in a painting gallery or a stable of vintage cars. Others prefer to keep their net worth a total secret, even to their banker, let alone their neighbors. Some people like to get totally emotionally involved with their "investments," prehaps using a hobby computer to analyze and intensively work with them. Others want a totally "hands-off" approach in which they let things sit and don't want to spend any personal time at all on them.

In any case, you have to match what you call your "investments" to your attitudes toward them. You will almost certainly do better in an "investment" that matches your personal needs than you will do continually fighting and fretting over something that just isn't right-vibed for you.

Investments— ante up enough to play the game

Each traditional "investment" has a minimum or cover charge to keep the riff raff out. Unless you can ante up enough to play the game on the big boy's terms, the extra commissions, odd-lot charges, minimum balances, margin calls, deposits, points, and so on will eat you alive.

Some minimums:

* $2500 in stocks at a discount broker house
* $5000 in bonds
* Ten bullion coins, usually $1200—$2000.
* 10% for a real estate down payment

If you can't meet the minimum, save up till you do. A round trip commission on a $500 stock trade will cost you around ten percent, *plus* the odd lot charges, *plus* the bid-ask differential. The round trip on a $2500 stock trade is around two percent, one fifth as much. The commission on a single bond may be $24, while you can get five bonds for $5 each, or only $25. (These are discount broker figures; ripoff old-line brokers may charge two or three times more.)

Needless to say, always find out how much extra you have to pay in "low end" expenses in any "investment." If you can't make the grade, don't try it.

Investments—research is essential

The more *accurate* information you can possibly get on any "investment," the better your odds of gaining by it. The trouble with information on most investments is that . . .

* much of it is nothing but blind hope
* a lot of it consists of outright lies
* insiders get theirs first
* profit is made selling you information
* most of it is outrageously overpriced
* it is often discounted before you can use it

About the only truly reliable information you can cheaply secure on any "investment" is its past price history. Even this isn't too useful when the markets are open, but on weekends when everything sits still for you, at least you have current and accurate information. Since past price history is about the only thing you can be absolutely sure of in an "investment," it makes sense to base your decisions heavily on this information.

Be highly suspect of traditional investment research. Some of the bad guys to avoid:

* **Company Annual Reports** are simply self-serving, ego-reinforcing bullshit. They heavily disguise reality. One I got recently proudly stated, "Our best third quarter ever!" The truth was that the bottom fell out of the sales since the previous quarter and disaster was impending. There is ONE very useful piece of information in an annual report. This is the address to send for your copy of the company's *10K report*. All you do is write the clown listed and tell him you are a stockholder and you will get a copy of the 10K. The 10K report tells exactly what the company is doing, who is suing them, all patent fights, all economic clouds on their horizon, and all the bad news, placed accurately, concisely, and unemotionally.

10K reports are also available from reprint services that list in the financial papers.

* **Investment Advisory Services**—These are sort of like the monthly caving grotto newsletters, except the printing quality and writing style is usually worse, the price is 100 to 1000 times higher, and the investment information they provide is much less useful.

* **Professional Financial Managers**—Gack. Some very interesting studies have repeatedly shown that professional money managers and institutions usually turn out investment decisions that are worse than totally random "dartboard" style decisions. The mess they have made of the Dow and most pension funds drives this home. The meaning is simply this—you are better off having a blindfolded baboon pick your "investment" strategy for you than this professional help. In fact, things have gotten so bad, the pros have *admitted* being worse than blindfolded baboons, and have introduced a new concept called *indexing*. With indexing, the pros promise to faithfully try and do as good as blindfolded baboons in the future. So far the results are mixed.

* **Stock Brokers**—There are two types of stock brokerage houses, the *discount broker* and the *ripoff broker*. A discount broker gets paid by the hour to take your order and politely execute it for you as cheaply as possible. He will in no way interfere with your investment decisions. A ripoff broker gets paid by how much money he can con you into investing. He will also charge you two or three times as much in commissions for this privilege. He also will spoon feed you "research" intended to (1) increase further his outrageous commissions, and (2) bestow upon you the deceased cats and dogs his smarter clients have recently flushed. Practically all the old-line stock houses are ripoff brokers, especially the name brand biggies. The research you get from a discount broker (none at all) will most often be better than what you get from a ripoff broker. Discount houses advertise in *Barrons, Wall Street Journal,* and other financial magazines.

Investments—selling is everything

Any idiot can buy into an "investment" at any time. That is not the problem. The key problem is deciding when to sell an "investment" and when to take a profit from it.

Everything goes against you when it is time to sell:

* Your profit is skyrocketing and "waiting just a little longer make you even more. Sure.

* Your broker or whatever is doing everything he can do to keep you from selling out, since, once the herd starts the other way, he is in deep trouble.

* Even with an absolute disaster, maybe, by just waiting, your investment's bankruptcy, class action litigation, the patent fight, and stockholder's suit is resolved, things will swing back to intrinsic goodness and you can ride off into the sunset on your Lancia with a Moog synthesizer on your back.

* Maybe you need cash NOW, and there is no choice.

* Even the concept that investments are for the dark distant future, for the "long pull" is fighting you.

Selling is the problem. One of the first things you should do when you get your own investment program rolling is to **practice selling things as soon and as fast as you possibly can.** Get into the timing. Make mistakes. Try to become objective and unemotional about selling timing. **Set rules and stick by them.**

Above all, time your selling to maximize your returns, rather than selling when you desperately need cash.

If you are going to need a bunch of cash sometime next year, sell out of the things where timing is crucial as far ahead as you can. Switch into T-bills or some short-term "investment" that is very liquid and does not have critical timing involved with it. If you must dump something, pick the "investment" with the *least* potential or the *least* return, not the one showing the most gain. Unless, of course, your timing tells you that now is the selling hour anyway.

diversify your "investments"

Otherwise known as not putting all your eggs in one basket. Nuff said.

have targeted "investments"

Remember how we said that minimizing any and all fixed obligations of your money machine is a major goal? Wouldn't it be nice if you could completely eliminate all utility bills, insurance premiums, and so on? If there only was a way.

But there is. It is called *targeting*.

And it is super simple. *Buy into the companies that are ripping you off.* For instance, if you have a $50 per month power bill, buy utility stocks or bonds that pay you $50 a month in interest or dividends back. You've just worked out a deal that says, "I'll lend you some money, you lend me some electricity." Only, you can get your money back anytime you want. Their electricity is gone forever.

This obviously will also work with the phone company and water people. As we've already seen, the same idea is the third best route to free life insurance as well.

A *targeted* investment is one that has a specific purpose. It generates a specific amount of money to offset or solve some money machine obligation.

Targeting does lots of good things for you. It is an automatic hedge and diversification. It can eliminate your fixed expenses. It can have tax advantages since the income and outgo offset each other. And, you get your initial investment *back* when the game is over.

Use targeting as a relatively small part of your overall "investment" picture. But use it aggressively to eliminate or provide for as many fixed money machine obligations as you can. Even if the loop isn't directly closed in the same company, using one investment to provide a source of needed income for some other obligation is a very good way to keep things profitable and orderly.

how I make a killing on Wall Street without shooting a broker

OK, so much for the theory. Here is something that seems to be working for me. It seems to be doubling my pre-tax money every year. It's a method with a medium amount of gamble, hassle, and risk. It takes a reasonable amount of time, say, an hour per week. It is suited for extra nickels that are to be multiplied.

The game is simply intermediate term trading of stocks through a discount broker. The stocks are usually held around six weeks or so. There is no intent other than selling the stocks for more than was paid for them. Two things have recently made intermediate term trading more attractive. These are the much lower commissions offered by the discount brokers, and the uncertainty and lengthening of capital gains tax treatment to where a few months won't help any.

I call the method the *MFQD extractor*. Which stands for *matched filter/quadrature demodulator*, its electronic analog. It's based on an electronic principle that says that the more you know about a signal, the easier it is to extract it out of deep noise. The signal in this case is a cyclic price variation in a stock that lasts one earnings period, and the extraction is designed to suck it dry and put it in your piggy bank.

The theory behind all this goes something like this. I feel that stock price variations are *not quite* random. The actual price is determined mostly by whether there are more buyers or sellers at any particular hour. But there are some very definite unrandomizing effects at work:

* On a thinly traded stock, *any* buy or sell drives the price away from its perceived value.

* The commissions and other charges introduce a threshold effect that prevents very short or very tiny buys and sells.

* There is an "attention getting" factor where more and more people will take a profit when the price goes up, and more and more people will be tempted to buy or average down as the price drops.

* There's simply the fact that true randomness takes lots and lots of data, and a few random events will typically cluster and behave vastly non-random.

These are obvious. It is also rather obvious that the condition of the company and the condition of the economy will have long-term effects on the average price.

But the far and away biggest non-randomizing effect is the one we are going to tap. *Stocks have a price history personality that is determined by who is buying and selling the stock and their motivations in doing so.*

The obvious key is to pick stocks whose personality fit the signal you are trying to extract from them. The pattern we are after is a stock that is generally rising rather slowly but that has four or so steep cycles in the recent price history.

To use this method, I keep a continuous plot of the weekly price of selected stocks against time. The plotting is done on semi-log paper so that all changes and percentage profits are comparable. To find the stocks in the first place, four or so times a year, I pick up a good chart service. The cheapest and far away the best I've found are the rather crappy looking *Quote NY, Quote American,* and *Quote OTC,* usually available around $5 each from

Harry Lankford
Box 213
Wichita, KA, 67201

I also get an obscure financial advisory service called the *Los Angeles Times*. This is used to update the charts and costs far less than most other sources of stock prices.

When you look at these personality histories, you'll find some just plain dull stocks that don't change price much. You'll find a few obvious winners that are temporarily skyrocketing, and lots of losers in a long term nosedive. You'll find some stocks whose variations are so erratic and random that, no way, can you find a rule that lets you make a profit on them.

You'll also find some stocks with neat cyclic variations, buy variations that are too slight to make a profit on after you allow for the commissions and any OTC bid-ask differential.

But, and this is the key point, if you look very close you will find a tidy collection of stocks that are nicely cyclic, going through one cycle of 30% or so price change once each quarter. Maybe one stock in twenty will meet this personality test.

An absolutely ideal stock for the MFQD Extractor looks like this:

* Its long-term average is gently upwards, say 15% per year.

* It is an obscure and thinly traded stock, having only a few hundred to a few thousand shares sold per day.

* There are some very recent and well-defined cycles with a 30% or so variation and not much noise messing them up.

* There are zero or very few institutional holdings.

* The past history of earnings is reasonably good. No deficits, and preferably the black dot that means earnings are up each year for the last five.

* The Price/Earnings ratio is reasonably low, meaning the stock is based on produced value, rather than blind hope

and finally . . .

* The stock is in a company whose products you don't feel bad about.

You'll find good candidates on the American exchange. Some obvious ones will jump out at you from the OTC market, but once you subtract out the stiff bid-ask differential, these may not be as attractive. I've used the method successfully on all three exchanges.

After a preliminary sort to find some candidates, you then go to a pocket calculator or a handy-dandy home computer. You then ask the question "What is the best *single* rule I could have used to make a profit on this beast over the last year?"

The stocks that come up with an answer something like "Buy when the price *drops* 20% from a fairly wide high; *sell* when the price goes 10% above your break-even" are the ones you want. You then check the stocks with a rule like this for their overall profit, as well as their annual rate of return. You also check for the uniformity and reasonableness of the cycles.

Now, if a certain stock obeyed this rule exactly, you would make ten percent on a trade. All this risk for a lousy ten percent.

But wait. Do this four times a year and the ten percent compounds to a 44 percent return. And since you are only in the stock half the time or less, two 44-percent returns together give you a 100-percent return or an annual doubling. This is after all commissions and charges but before taxes and inflation.

Even the ten percent isn't all that bad, since it's better than you can do with a lot of "investments." Better yet, you most often get more than ten percent, since this is the trigger point. I've had a stock go up 70 percent on the way past the trigger. And, you are likely to be in the stock for less than half the time with reasonable luck.

The method assumes there will be one more cycle along after you buy in. Most often this is the case. You keep updating your selections as the personalities of the stocks gradually change.

I normally buy the stocks in even hundred lots to bring the total close to but above $2500, the best price break on the discount curve. Very low priced stocks are avoided, particularly on the OTC market. I always make sure that there are lots of unhappy people stuck with the stock when I buy in on the 20% drop. Very brief "flash-in-the-pan" peaks are treated as impulse noise and are ignored. Very expensive stocks are also avoided.

I do all this on weekends. Everytime I get in a hurry and try something mid-week, it costs me money. I've also tried using limits with dismal results. No shorts are involved. Dividends are ignored. No margin is used, but the stock earnings are shuttled back and forth to a savings account as timing dictates. All orders are placed first thing Monday morning.

Naturally, you buy at a low and sell when the expected increase is met. Your charts should include a 100% annual return slope line to keep your investment goal in sight.

Should a disaster strike, the stock is averaged down on an additional 20 percent drop. Twice now, I haven't had the gall to do this, and twice I lost all sort of potential profit by not doing so on the upswing that followed.

The hardest thing is to set rules and follow them, rather than working on hunches or gut feelings. When you find something that seems to work for you, *believe in it faithfully.*

Several more details. You do the exact opposite of "conventional" stock market wisdom. *Nail down your profits immediately and let your losses ride.* The longer a profit sits there, the more likely someone else will grab it before you can. Letting a loser sit may do no harm if you trade a possible future breakeven or gain for a certain immediate loss. Another important rule is to *buy only stocks that are decreasing in price* and *sell only stocks that are increasing in price.* Don't chase an already moving stock or try to catch the peak or trough.

A final and key detail is to *have your stock market activity be the exact opposite of everyone else's.* Remember that all investments are cyclical. When the market is near an all time high, there is no reasonable way to make further profits, so GET OUT! Use the Dow as a guide. If the last Dow long term high was 1000 and the last disaster dip was 600, set rules that reduce your involvement with increasing market index values. For instance, between 600 and 700 buy heavily and take only large profits. Between 700 and 800 buy more cautiously while taking more modest profits more often. Between 800 and 900 be extremely uptight with any new money and take smaller profits yet more often. From 900 to 920, don't buy anthing at all. Above 920, GET OUT. Wait till the inevitable swingback and start over.

No way will I say the MFQD extractor will work for you or will work all the time. I only claim that it is working for me now. Of some twenty-five transactions to date, all have been profitable except for a $7 loss because I got in a hurry and a locked-in dog that started me in this game in the first place. Even the dog was eventually dumped at a $500 profit. Average return on cash flow has been nearly 100 percent annually, before taxes and inflation.

The obvious disadvantages of the MFQD extractor are that you are often out of a stock when it makes a long term up-move, are possibly into a stock when it is dropping radically, and you have a relatively low payoff expectation for the risk involved. It also takes raw guts to buy when everyone else is selling and vice versa.

But, it seems to work. If all this cubic goodness keeps up, of course, I'll write a book on it. There's far more return in writing books than there ever will be in playing the stock market. The use of home computers to make this whole process more accurate and more profitable yet is obvious.

invest in the incredible secret money machines of others

Well, we've come a long, long way. Once again, everything I've said so far is my opinion and my belief in things that are working for me and my money machine, along with my perceptions of what seems to be working for the secret money machines of others.

I've probably hacked off some people who make money off things I don't feel are important in secret money machines. But, perhaps, I have motivated several someones for every person I may have displeased. Hopefully, some of you out there in readerland see that a very profitable incredible secret money machine can be yours and can return a tremendous amount of profit for very little invested. This is done through our keys of a total lifestyle commitment to a small-scale computer, craft, or technical business; a low profile, low-hassle approach; careful control of communications; and leading with a maximum amount of personal value added.

Its your turn now. You can try out what seems to agree with you and what seems to be workable for you. But, don't believe a word of this. Prove it to yourself, and ripoff only what will work for you.

And, if you like what you accomplish—help others do the same.

Don't miss the egress!

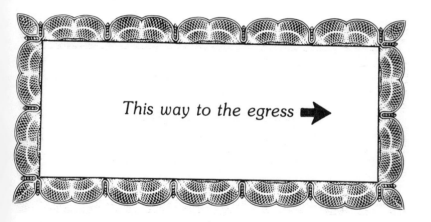

This way to the egress ➡

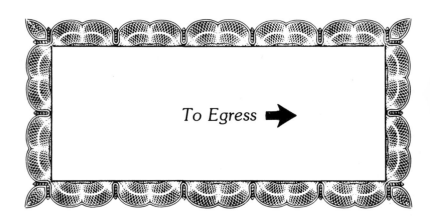